"A holistic approach to routine issues in life"

JUST A POINT
Musings at dawn

DALJIT SINGH UTAAL   **GURPREET SINGH WANDER**

INDIA • SINGAPORE • MALAYSIA

ISBN
Paperback 979-8-89610-655-5
Hardcase 979-8-89699-337-7

Photographs by:
Harpreet Singh Sandhu
Former Additional Advocate General, Punjab
and
A Nature Artist.

We are indebted to our parents, spouse, children, friends, colleagues and family for supporting us wholeheartedly.

DECLARATION

The proceeds from sales of this book will be used to distribute free copies among college and senior school students to promote holistic personal development in our youth.

Preface

This book has come about in a unique and interesting manner. It is a compilation of thoughts which are based on free and frank discussions that we have had during our regular morning walks over the last 30 years. A variety of issues were deliberated upon for 30 - 40 minutes each. These were not just theoretical concepts but were real life issues which we come across every day, triggered by happenings in our family, professional and social life. Over a period, we realised that we were reaching a reasonably good inference and started noting down the gist of it on returning home. The points were neither structured nor planned and were randomly arranged since that is how they occurred during our walks.

Most of what we have expressed may already be known to you. We are aware that the messages are not great pearls of wisdom, nor are they any secrets of success. However, surely, they are relevant issues of any present-day professional's daily life. Our opinions may not be applicable and appropriate for all situations. However, they will trigger a thought process in your mind in the context of related circumstances. We have provided a nidus to initiate a process of contemplation, which is necessary because at times all of us take things for granted and keep acting reflexly without giving adequate attention.

What comes to your mind may at times be different from what has been written by us. Many of you will have better ideas and solutions. The purpose of this book is to make you think about day-to-day issues for a while, and dwell upon the best ways of dealing with them.

A daily dose will help you to reflect and have a better insight. It will empower you to act consciously and take the way forward with greater awareness. These ground realities are not rules but are tools, timeless tips and points of views that have emerged after a lot of straight talk and discussion during our morning walks.

We have presented pointed tips on very diverse issues and situations. As doctors, we have included health-related suggestions on meditation, exercise, sleep, and a balanced diet. Work related passing shots deal with skill development, leadership, teamwork, culture of the workplace and how to deal with seniors, colleagues, and juniors. There are positive strokes on balance in life, self-development, awareness, time and stress management, work-home balance, and positive mind control. We never wanted the message to be too lengthy and have deliberately kept them brief to facilitate easy readability. There is no relationship between the picture, the date, and the thought. The combination only provides an identity to a single thought for focus, one day at a time, preferably to be deliberated upon in the early morning since that is when our mind is fresh and not cluttered by the day's events.

The ideas are mostly simple and mundane, but they are original. One rarely sees a book of this kind dealing with a variety of such elementary but important issues. We have enjoyed and learned a lot throughout the process of penning and polishing the manuscript. In fact, after finalizing the contents when we now talk about a random subject, we often realize that it already features in our book.

We hope you will enjoy reading the book. Reflect on the messages in the context of your day-to-day life. We assure you there will not be a moment of boredom or getting stuck up while reading. The remarkable feature is that you may spend just 5 minutes at a time or, if you wish, read it like a regular book. We feel you may find it more enjoyable and interesting to go through the points one by one.

We are thankful to our families for their support during the compilation of these thoughts. We could reach a consensus on all the points with ease since both of us are from similar service class science background and both are experienced clinicians, teachers, and administrators. There is great mutual respect and understanding, and consequently this book is the result of a unique two author consensus with regular contributions from our spouses. We would like to thank our friends who gave critical feedback and those who provided scenic pictures of the morning time which is consistent with the background of the book. The publishers have done a great job in presenting the material in a beautiful manner.

We have authored several medical books, but this is our first book on general life issues. Feedback from the readers will be highly appreciated and will help us to polish the subject matter for the second edition, whenever it comes out. We are thankful to Muskan Sharma for helping us to shape the book and providing us with many photographs. We thank Jagjeet Singh Bajwa for helping us in the latter half after Muskan went to the USA. But without Muskan and Jagjeet this book would not have been possible.

Dr. Gurneet Chinna and Dr. Harpal Singh also provided us with photographs from their collection. Most of the photographs are courtesy Harpreet Sandhu who is a good friend and has a keen interest in photography.

We present this book to you with humility and respect.

Daljit Singh Utaal   Gurpreet Singh Wander

Spend some time in solitude

In the hustle bustle of life, we may forget the value of being with just ourselves. Spend some quality time contemplating every day. Communicate with the inner self and review what right and wrong one is doing.

Solitude is quite different to loneliness. It is a period of spiritual cleansing that makes the mind clear and peaceful.

Keep a balance in life

Everything is good only in moderation. Most of us have multiple roles and responsibilities. Excessive involvement in one thing occupies us fully and the balance is lost.

Too much pursuit of a particular activity makes us obsessed with it and compromises other important ones.

A long walk frees the mind!

Indulging in mundane physical activities like taking a long walk may give the erroneous impression that it is just mechanical. On the contrary, it allows the mind to go into a wandering state which, though restful, encourages free thinking and imagination.

Creative ideas emerge in a facilitative environment.

Remain in good company

We tend to acquire the good and bad attributes of the people we spend most of our time with. The company we keep can have a great influence on our views, priorities, ambitions and motivation. The peer effect is significant, more so at a young age.

One should choose companions who are ethical, skilled, honest and sincere.

Holistic Health is desirable!

To be healthy, pay attention to all its components: physical (regular exercise, healthy food), mental (control on mind and emotions), spiritual (faith in God, knowing self, having compassion, shunning vices) and social (being in sync with society, following norms and systems, being pleasant and acceptable).

Health is multidimensional and all its aspects are important.

Have the right diet

A balanced diet is essential for good health. It is recommended to consume a diet rich in fruits, vegetables, nuts, whole grains, low fat milk products and foods high in protein (pulses, whole gram, beans, fish and egg white).

Avoid sugar, ghee, trans fats, high salt preserved foods, egg yolk and red meat.

Tame the mind

The mind is a good slave but a bad master. It is restless, wandering and uninhibited by nature. Left on its own, it is like a wild animal and can disrupt rational thinking.

Taming the mind and bringing it under control is tough but is surely within our power. One has to make an effort for it.

Extreme emotions indicate lack of balance

Some people become dejected and despondent when things do not go their way. At other times they are ecstatic and overjoyed over some positive happenings. Either way, they overreact, lose focus and thus waste time and energy.

A balanced person can handle the vicissitudes of life without too much effect on the psyche.

Stay away from addictions

Addiction is related not just to drugs and intoxicants. When we cannot abstain from an activity by choice, we are addicted. Since it is compulsive, it prevents us from balancing our other important activities.

Any addiction can become irresistible and start controlling the individual. Break it before it breaks us.

Real relaxation does not come from devices

People often carry the impression that entertainment with an electronic device relaxes the brain. In fact, such an activity may paradoxically lead to mental fatigue and exhaustion as it consumes a lot of energy.

'Switching off' mentally and freedom from thoughts is the way to bring the brain to a resting mode.

Collect full information before making decisions

We initially have some impressions regarding an issue, then we form opinions, and based on these we take decisions. Our opinions can be erroneous if the information is incomplete.

Do not rush in to draw conclusions or pass judgements before the six cardinal questions about an issue are answered: What, When, Where, Who, Why and How?

Adopt a comprehensive fitness program

The human body is built for movement and physical activity. Fitness regimes should include the 4 Ss-stamina, strength, suppleness and speed. Regular exercise covering each of these components needs to be part of daily routine, at all ages.

A range of exercises, in an appropriate proportion according to age, is required to maintain overall physical fitness.

Just do it

'Well begun is half done' is a popular maxim. It gives an important message because it emphasizes making a good beginning. However, the pressure of doing well often dissuades us from taking up a challenging task and we tend to postpone it.

Do not dwell on how good the beginning is. The first step overcomes inertia and facilitates the next one, setting us on the path.

Keep asking "why"

Analysis of a problem entails answering a series of questions. We tend to avoid doing this because the process is painstaking, but the effort spent is certainly worth it. The solution to any troublesome issue becomes simple and easy if we understand the rationale for it.

Great ideas, discoveries and inventions have emerged from relentless questioning.

Note down your thoughts

At times a good idea can get lost if one does not note it down. Ideas often come in flashes and may not appear again. Recording important thoughts enables us to retrieve them in the future. Even a key word or phrase is enough.

The raw text can be polished later. New thoughts will emerge later and help us to take the idea forward.

What looks easy may not actually be so

When we witness an expert executing an act in a seemingly easy manner, it may not be realized that the performance is the result of long experience and intense practice. The 'effort' that has gone into making it appear 'effortless' is not apparent. If we try doing it ourselves, we will understand how difficult it is.

Learn the secret of making tough tasks look simple.

Learn to say "no"

An offer or invitation may seem to be a favor. However, it could have arisen from the other person's need and not be of particular interest to you. By accommodating every request, one may be putting an unnecessary burden on time and energy. Ask yourself if it is worth it.

A polite "no" is much better than trying to please others at one's own expense.

All mistakes do not deserve punishment

If a subordinate makes a mistake at work, corrective action needs an analysis of the reason. In case the exact expectation was not clear to the person, provide orientation and information. If the error was due to time constraint or lack of expertise, give guidance and training. Both the grounds are excusable.

Punitive action is required only for wrong acts done deliberately.

Think like a child but act like an adult

Children do not know what is right or wrong and are unaware of the consequences of their actions. At the same time, they have a wild and uninhibited imagination. Such unrestricted thinking creates more ideas and possibilities and allows a wide range of options.

Have the creativity of a child but analyze the alternatives in a mature and rational way.

Do not break a good partnership

Successful partnerships involve combination of different skills which are complementary to each other. The combined output may far exceed the sum of the individual performances. Such associations should be nurtured and sustained because the results often decline significantly when the partnership splits.

Breaking a good collaboration may be disastrous!

Learn by observing others

Appreciate the exceptional qualities of others and try to emulate them. Of course, many variables like natural ability, circumstances and luck cannot be replicated. However, factors like effort, training, practice and gaining deep knowledge of the concerned field are within one's control.

Instead of being jealous, try to acquire the good qualities of others.

Be gentle, but not weak!

Being gentle and polite is a good attribute but may sometimes be mistaken for weakness. People tend to take a person with a soft nature for granted.

If anyone takes advantage of your gentleness, it may be worth taking a tough approach and deliberately giving a glimpse of 'what you can do' even if you are not aggressive or dominating by nature.

Resolve a conflict with tact

Trying to resolve a conflict with anger, hostility or threat is counterproductive. A spiral of increasing tension ensues, causing escalation of the dispute. Even if the other person acts in an unreasonable manner, it is better to remain calm and rational.

One needs to handle sensitive situations tactfully and not respond aggressively to provocative behavior.

We are what we deserve to be

Many factors determine how we progress in life, like education, intelligence, attitude, caliber, diligence, support system, circumstances and fate. An occasional failure can be attributed to bad luck but one cannot keep blaming destiny for every setback.

Eventually all the variables even out and one becomes what one ought to be.

Do not compare with others

Some of the qualities we possess may be as good as or even better than the attributes of people who are otherwise better placed or more successful in the eyes of the world. Every individual lives his own life and comparisons are not good.

One should be proud of the self-virtues and need not be bothered about the others.

Do not allow emotional blackmail by children

Small children learn emotional blackmail by default. They get their desires fulfilled by displaying distress or throwing tantrums, banking on the soft attitude of their parents and grandparents.

Do not accept unreasonable demands of the child, otherwise the tendency to take advantage soon becomes a habit.

Accept the ups and downs of life

No state is perpetual. What goes up must come down, and the other way round. When an extreme is reached, the only way possible is the other direction. The vicissitudes of life must be accepted, and it is sensible to take everything in stride.

Avoid arrogance when one is up, and despair when one is down.

Act on the short term

Think far but act near. We should be clear where we want to go. However, the immediate hurdles and blocks need attention rather than remote, vague and often unfounded perceptions of problems.

Like the headlights of a car, focus on the things lying directly in front of you, rather than fretting about distant ones.

Let the subconscious mind solve a problem

Sometimes solutions to vexing problems do not come while we are single-mindedly concentrating on them. In such situations, just let the conscious mind sit back. Move on to something else. The 'aha' moment may come later.

The subconscious mind takes it up and eventually comes up with the solution, when one is in a relaxed state.

Teamwork brings success

A team functions successfully when people with different skills come together and contribute in their own way. Individually, each one may not be that effective. All the members should be assigned roles which they are best equipped to handle so as to complement each other's strengths.

A good leader is one who can get the team into a cohesive unit act as a force multiplier.

Mastering a skill needs hard work

Sheer brilliance is not enough to master a skill. Persistent practice is equally important. We may be born gifted, but converting potential into actual ability requires resolute effort.

There is no short cut to achievement. Competence and expertise come only with diligence and hard work!

READERS NOTE

One is both a student and a teacher

Learning is a continuous process throughout life. We keep learning things from others in some way or the other, irrespective of their age, status and occupation. At the same time, other people directly or indirectly learn from us, even if we may not be formally teaching them.

Every person is a student and a teacher at the same time.

Learn from other's mistakes

As we carry out our work, it is natural to make errors. It is good to learn from our mistakes and avoid repeating them. However, it is even better to critically observe others and note their mistakes so that they can be avoided in the first place.

We do not have to commit every mistake ourselves before we learn.

Keep your calm even with nasty people

We need to deal with unpleasant people on many occasions. It is natural to have a feeling of disgust, and one may detest their company. Make a deliberate effort to stay positive and avoid getting upset. Do not stoop to their level by responding in the same manner as they behave.

It is better to stay away than getting stuck with such people.

Reason for irrational behavior!

A person who acts unreasonably in the 'heat of the moment' because of overwhelming circumstances needs sympathy rather than criticism. However, if there is breakdown of self-control on a regular basis, we must make it clear to the offender that it will not be acceptable.

We must try to understand the context and reason for someone's irrational behavior and respond accordingly.

Play your part as a mentor

As we grow older, our responsibility to act as a mentor increases. Maturity and wide experience enable us to provide good advice to youngsters. However, we should avoid imposing our ideas on them.

Setting examples and becoming a role model is a more acceptable and effective approach to guide young people.

Other's problems may be complex

The different aspects and exact circumstances of another person's problems can never be perfectly gauged by us. How, then, can our simplistic solutions solve a complex problem which we do not even fully understand?

At best, we can provide information and our personal viewpoint which may help deal with someone's problem.

Don't forget the
self-resolutions!

We all make new year and birthday resolutions, like losing weight, getting rid of certain habits, finishing some projects etc. However, the motivation peters off after a few days and we are back to routine. One can link it with the same date every month and use it as a reminder.

Create your own method to remember the self-resolutions!

Select what to do first

Prioritization is the key to handling multiple tasks. Selecting the proper sequence is an important factor for the best outcome. The easier, more important and impactful things with a 'felt need' should be tackled first.

Early success provides satisfaction. The other more complex issues can then be taken up with confidence.

Resolve conflicts early

The key to resolving a conflict is to sort it out as early as possible, even if it means bending a bit. Do not let ego, pride or arrogance complicate matters and get in the way of early settlement.

As disputes get prolonged, they tend to get complicated, and it becomes more and more difficult to sort out the issues.

Infobesity is counterproductive

Good decision-making is possible only when we are able to think clearly and are equipped with just the right amount of authentic and appropriate information.

Too much detail makes it difficult to assess and analyze facts in a rational manner. This can result in confusion and is counter-productive.

A setback might be an opportunity

We must never get overly dejected or upset when an adverse event happens. It may seem that nothing good can come out of the situation, but it is difficult to anticipate how life will unfold.

Sometimes seemingly unfortunate events may be a blessing in disguise and offer an opportunity to do something with a better outcome.

Expertise in a specific skill

In every field of work there is a range of activities that need to be performed. For professional success, it is a good idea to pick out a particular component one is good at. Spend extra time to master the skill.

As we become proficient in a specific area of work, the expertise gets recognized, and the beneficiaries gravitate towards us.

Changing beliefs is very difficult

Strong convictions are difficult to shed off. For some people, irrefutable proof is required to alter their beliefs, and such evidence is often difficult to come by. Reasoning and logic may or may not help to convince such people.

Try to change anyone's convictions only if you must.

Love needs to be expressed

One should not assume that love and affection are obvious and need not be expressed in established relationships. They too demand affirmation and consolidation. Even close bonds cannot be taken for granted and must be constantly reinforced.

Love and affection need to be communicated through word and action.

Do not lose sight of distant goals

We often tend to postpone tasks that are less pressing but more important. Sometimes routine engagements keep us occupied and we do not realize that we are not working for the goals which may be distant but are more significant in the long term.

Prioritize the goals and divide the time accordingly.

Feedback must be genuine

True feedback can be obtained only from our real well-wishers. No one can be trusted more than our own parents, spouse or offspring. They may appear to be unduly critical, but the sentiments and observations are genuine.

Only authentic feedback is of any use.

First impressions can be misleading

Things and issues may not be as simple as they first appear to be. Conversely, apparently complex things may be quite simple. Do not jump to conclusions on face value. Careful, continuous and critical observation will reveal the true nature of things, issues and people.

Proper analysis helps to interpret the situation and make a correct judgement.

Adopt new techniques at an appropriate stage

When a new technique is introduced in the profession, do not rush in, to take it up immediately. In the early stage it is likely to be insufficiently defined and more cumbersome. On the other hand, those who leave it too late will be left behind others in the field.

Look for the right time to adopt new technology, neither too early nor too late.

Enjoy the positive ride

In a project that is going well, sometimes we may feel it can be changed and made even better. Do not spoil things by trying to tinker too much with it! There are many unseen factors in a successful system.

It is better to enjoy the ride and let it run smoothly with gradual improvements rather than making radical changes.

Take difficult tasks head on

If a tough and vexatious part of our job bothers us but cannot be avoided, it is better to grab it by the horns. It will gradually become easier. A half-hearted and tentative approach only makes the difficulty appear worse.

If we keep on postponing some work because it appears difficult, it may be too late and then we would repent later.

The world sees what the person shows

We can only observe that aspect of a person which is presented to us, even though what is apparent may not be a true reflection of the character and personality. A few people reveal their deficiencies but many exhibit good behavior and confidence to cover their faults.

Do not be misled by casual impressions about people.

Having a goal gives direction

Success implies attaining a predetermined goal. Our energies get directed when there is an objective. A clear target motivates us to take steps to reach it.

It is possible that we may fall short of the goal in spite of our best efforts. However, if there is no idea where we wish to go, we will reach nowhere!

Some attributes have a duality

The same word can have different connotations according to the situation in which it is used. Attributes cannot be categorically declared as good or bad. For example, when we describe someone as proud, strict, aggressive, hard, flexible, indulgent etc., it can denote a positive or negative quality, depending on the context.

The circumstances and conditions must be kept in mind while we interpret an attribute.

Support friends proactively

Sometimes people in difficulty or distress avoid sharing their burden. We should not wait for a friend to seek help. Once we know that he or she is grappling with a problem, we must take the initiative and provide whatever assistance, moral support and counseling is possible.

All of us need support in difficult times. A friend in need is a friend indeed!

Be what you expect of others.

Managing oneself well is very important for maintaining good interpersonal relationships. Look within yourself and correct your own faults and flaws. We need to be caring and thoughtful about the feelings of others.

To be liked, one must be likeable. Sort yourself, and you will find that the relations with everyone will improve.

Just get started

Initial struggle is inherent to any enterprise. Ease and comfort must be sacrificed for the eventual good. While crossing a river, we need to let go of the shore to reach the other side.

Resolve and single-mindedness in boldly taking the first step is required. Self-doubt and confusion should be avoided.

Take note of common proverbial sayings

Well known quotations, sayings and proverbs are based on practical situations replicated many times over. They are popular and frequently cited because each one is time tested and universally applicable.

Acknowledging the relevance of quotes allows us to be aware of worldly wisdom and to learn important life lessons.

Avoid extremes of expressions

Science teaches us that nothing is absolute. Avoid using strong expressions like "This can never happen", or "I am 100 percent sure". This leaves no room for change. Preferable terms are "unlikely" or "probable".

We should not be too dogmatic about our opinions. One realizes this with age, maturity and experience.

Be grateful to your parents and teachers

We reap the benefits of the nurturing and support of our parents, teachers and well-wishers in our formative years. We may never have taken off, if that initial thrust had not been provided.

The head-start eliminates much of the time-consuming struggle we may otherwise have had to face in the beginning. Should we not be full of gratitude?

READERS NOTE

Have faith in your capabilities

We should be aware of our strengths and weaknesses. However, perception of a weakness is often exaggerated or just imagined. By thinking negatively, we start believing that shortcomings exist.

To tap our potential adequately, we must have faith in our strengths and eliminate doubts.

Take forward what you have inherited

Inheritance can give a boost to the feeling of security and present enhanced opportunities to pursue more ambitious and meaningful goals. However, effort is required by the offspring to value and maintain, if not build on, the platform gifted to them.

The progeny of a self-made man must not fritter away the advantage provided to them by taking things easy.

Talk about your problems to yourself

Problems remain unsolved when the mind is confused and unclear. It is a good idea to verbalize the issue to bring it into focus. Just talking to yourself, as if to another person, may be good enough.

Defining a problem by putting it in words helps in its resolution. The results can be amazing.

Maintain a healthy lifestyle

Good health is essential for enjoying life. We must spend time and effort to maintain it. A nutritious, low fat, high protein and low carbohydrate diet is required. Regular moderate intensity, aerobic physical exercise as well as yoga, meditation and relaxation should be incorporated in our daily schedule.

A calm mind in a physically fit body is a treasure.

Do your best and leave the rest

Effort and hard work are important determinants of success and achievement. However, circumstances beyond our control may dictate how things evolve.

While we must always put in our best, do not discount the element of chance and fate. When the time is right, everything falls in place!

Just get started

It is said that well begun is half done. 'Begun' itself can be regarded as half done! Even a false start is, after all, a start and can be corrected as one goes along.

When we undertake a journey, we may initially find ourselves moving in the wrong direction. Adjustment and re-orientation can be made. Not begun, on the other hand, is obviously never done!

Think and find the right solution

In the enthusiasm to solve problems, we often tend to rush in and make hasty decisions. We must curb this tendency and weigh the options carefully before coming to a conclusion.

Make sure that the 'solution' does not create a new set of problems. In addition, the solution must not be worse than the original problem!

Avoid the halo effect

We tend to label and categorize people based on our general impression about them. We start believing that everything about someone we like or idolize is good, while another person may be taken as bad in all respects. This concept leads to errors of judgement about specific aspects.

Blanket perception about a person is called the halo effect. We must avoid such bias and recognize positive and negative attributes as they actually exist.

Collaborative decision making is always better

Involve the stakeholders of a system (home, office, friend circle) in decision making. Deciding something on behalf of others, even if it is ostensibly in their interest, is not appropriate. One person may miss some of the aspects and factors.

Brainstorming and collective decisions are generally more appropriate and are always better accepted by all.

Two brains are better than one

Things can go wrong in a project at any stage. A single person may not be able to think diversely enough and may be too biased or occupied to notice little cues. We should have an open approach where everyone can give suggestions.

In a problematic situation, eliciting the opinion of others helps. We are likely to get ideas which never crossed our mind.

Be courageous, but with caution!

There is a thin line between boldness and recklessness. The mindset should always remain positive but undue risk-taking behavior can be dangerous. Be courageous and adventurous, but do not act in an irresponsible manner by throwing caution to the winds.

Confidence is a good attribute, but over-confidence is counter-productive.

We can only control our own mind

Much of what is happening around us is beyond our control. We need to identify the things we can change and confine our efforts to these. We can only take full charge of how we, not others, think and feel.

Trying to change something that is not in our hands can only lead to frustration.

Some traits are more important

Some people are successful, in spite of not demonstrating any features of excellence. If we look carefully, we will find that a particular trait is responsible for their achievement. The same applies to the unexpected failure of people who seem to have all the qualities for doing well.

There are multiple determinants for success, and some of these overrides the others.

Learn from the lives of achievers

Studying the lives of people who have extraordinary achievements in their field - science, art, religion, politics, sports, music, philosophy, literature or any other sphere, is a great learning method.

The story of accomplished people is a window to how their mind works and reveals the key to success.

The factors for success

The factors that determine success or failure include passion, diligence, perseverance, caliber, aptitude, behavior, communication skills, attitude, personality, sincerity, loyalty, compassionate nature and many more.

A person's distinctive attributes, singly or collectively, contribute to eventual success.

Introspect before blaming others

If anything goes wrong, we tend to find fault with others but often have a blind spot when it comes to accepting our own contribution to the issue. While making a critical assessment of a problematic situation, one's personal lapses must not be disregarded.

It is good to introspect before putting the blame on someone else.

Get modern but in moderation

The world is constantly changing. One has to accept this fact and adapt accordingly. A rigid attitude will leave us out of sync with what is modern. However, the adjustment should be gradual and in moderation, and not disruptive of the prevalent ways.

A slow change is more acceptable as it causes less stress.

Nurture and groom the subordinates

Our role towards a new subordinate is akin to that of a parent. There needs to be a gradual but definite shift from control to direction, and eventually to facilitation. The pace of this transition depends on how quickly the learner matures.

Juniors need to be groomed and not just left to learn on their own.

Whatever succeeds will be repeated

The feeling of pleasure from any action sets off the desire to do it again. If something 'works' or succeeds, it will be repeated. Unfortunately, this applies to undesirable acts too.

Habits are nothing but compulsive repetition of actions which have initially provided some sort of gratification.

Do not depend on others for happiness

If we depend on other people to keep us happy, we are in for disappointment. No one else is in charge of the state of our mind. Others can only provide comfort, pleasure and a good environment.

Happiness is an internal state which is beyond the power of any external influence.

How to make others agree

It is a challenge to make people see a point of view that is contrary to their own. Aggression and hostility produce resistance and are generally ineffective. Gentle persuasion with patience, restraint and empathy are more effective.

Disagreement is best handled with polite reasoning instead of argument.

Recognize what we cannot change

Some things may be within our power to change while others are not. Recognizing this distinction is critical. Making attempts to influence a situation that is beyond our control is futile and frustrating.

We need to focus only on things that we can, or should, take charge of.

Perception of control may be an illusion

Some things are apparently within our authority or control, like the family, home or even our physical body. This may not be so. We may not be able to exert influence over them beyond an extent.

It is only our mind, and the actions willed by it, that are truly under our command.

Overthinking causes unhappiness

We can remain peaceful and happy by thinking rationally and positively. However, overthinking can be counterproductive since we start imagining too many possibilities that have a remote chance of materializing.

Those who overthink have a potential risk of getting unhappy by harboring negative thoughts and are more vulnerable to sadness.

Allow the mind to slowly settle down

The mind is creative, but it can go haywire and out of control in challenging circumstances. Since there is no limit to thinking, an unbridled mind leads to confusion and chaos.

When facing a complex situation, one should allow the disparate thoughts to gradually be reconciled through quiet contemplation. A serene calmness gradually prevails, and the right answers emerge.

Remain simple

People with a complex and unpredictable personality are difficult to understand. They produce stress in all those who deal with them. A simple and straightforward person is, on the other hand, a good company.

For the benefit of everyone, including for your own self, try to remain uncomplicated, balanced and reasonable.

Anger is failure of self-control

Anyone who exhibits anger is harboring an unnecessary negative emotion which has been released. Like the bursting of a pipe, it shows that it was already under pressure before being manifest.

One can consciously avoid getting angry if one is really calm within. No amount of provocation can then precipitate anger.

Emotions do not arise from thoughts

Emotions have a subconscious basis, and do not necessarily result from rational thinking. In fact, they may actually arise contrary to what the mind desires. They are related to feelings in response to triggers which may not be obvious.

To understand emotions, we need to delve deeply and identify the hidden underlying basis.

Motivation is the key to better performance

Getting someone to do a job better becomes easier by making it more meaningful from his or her point of view. "What do I get out of this" or "How do I benefit" are closely related to motivation.

It is human nature that one tends to carry out tasks more willingly and enthusiastically if a gain is perceived.

Do not waste time on trivial issues

Recognize the futility of triviality. Do not be bothered about or get entangled in petty matters which have no significance or value in our life. Spending time and energy on things of little consequence is a waste.

Assess the importance of an issue before apportioning efforts to it.

Do not postpone important long-term issues

Problems can be divided in a 2 x 2 grid as acute/long-term, and important/unimportant. We tend to focus on issues immediately on hand simply because we think we will have time to deal with the ones which are not urgent, resulting in the latter being postponed indefinitely.

While deciding our actions, consideration should be based on the relative importance rather than the time frame.

READERS NOTE

Share your expertise

Some experts hesitate to impart their skills to others, as if they would create a competitor and lose their standing. Actually, when a skill is shared, it gets sharpened. Sharing expertise will enhance our value, not diminish it. The beneficiaries will respect us for it.

Do not let your skills and knowledge die with you.

Offer guidance without imposing your choice.

When we give advice to someone, we expect it to be followed. We tend to get disappointed and even upset if that does not happen. It must be realized that a suggestion cannot and should not be binding. There is no obligation on the person to accept our opinion and heed to our advice.

The final decision must rest with the recipient of advice because it is he or she who will bear the consequences.

We cannot really change anyone

Personality and habits are generally fixed. When it is so difficult to change our own self, we cannot expect to be able to manipulate or modify the basic nature of others, including near and dear ones. Even in a marriage, accepting the partner for who they are is the best way.

Changing someone is one of the most challenging tasks we can entrust to ourselves.

It is not easy to step in someone's shoes

At times we may be critical of someone and feel that we can do more justice to their work or role. Literally as well as figuratively, stepping into someone else's shoes is easier said than done.

It is only when we try to be in someone else's place do we realize the difficulties and challenges faced in that role.

Use tact to avoid an unacceptable task

If an unethical task is thrust upon us which our conscience does not allow us to undertake, yet cannot be refused, we can use a smart tactic to justify withdrawal.

By conveying that the task is complicated and confusing, we can create an impression that it is beyond our capacity. One may be able to wriggle out of the uncomfortable situation.

Set your own limits

We should set limits for everything we do and try to stick to them. This is true for entertainment, eating, relaxing, partying, vacationing and even for positive things like work and exercise. Curbs and checks bring a balance in life.

If we do not maintain some restrictions and control, we tend to get carried away with pleasurable activities and forget when to stop.

Do not take health for granted

Youngsters at times feel that they will always remain fit. Good habits like healthy food, exercise, yoga, meditation, positive thinking, preventing sleep deprivation and watching weight and fitness levels should be inculcated from a young age.

A healthy lifestyle from a young age is an investment for good health and longevity.

Some compulsive activities are positive

Some compulsive activities and traits are harmless and may even have a positive impact on our life, for example punctuality, a creative urge, or a health-promoting pursuit.

There is no need to curb positive habits, unless they take up too much time or are at the expense of other important activities and interpersonal relationships.

One can contribute at any age

As long as mental faculties are intact, physical infirmity need not be a deterrent to productive living. Even as age advances, one should keep learning and contributing. Ask yourself: "How can I do even better" and "How could I help improve things around me"

One can be of service to the family and to society at any age.

The work desk tells a lot

We do not need a long period of observation to identify whether someone is disciplined and well ordered. Just look at the desk he or she occupies. At a glance one can get a fairly good idea about the working style of the person.

A tidy and properly laid out desk reflects a well-organized and methodical individual.

'Too many options' can be a problem

Unfortunate is the person who has no options, but he too has a problem who has too many choices. Facing multiple alternatives and different courses of action increases the potential of making mistakes through dilemma and confusion.

A clear thought process is required for good decision-making. Narrow down the options to make it easy.

Have a clear decision making strategy

Decision making is based on both subjective and objective considerations. If we know what exactly we want, the exercise is easier. At the same time, we need to have sufficient information about each alternative in terms of its pros and cons.

Make sure that decisions are based on facts and not merely on impressions.

Be flexible if the situation changes

What may appear to be the correct decision could have a different hue at a later time. It is wise to be flexible in the face of changed circumstances. Reconsider an earlier opinion if it is felt that an error has been made and revision is required.

Stubbornness, rigidity and ego can be damaging in the long run.

Be humble

Good performance backed by humility exudes charm and value. Modesty is an appreciated trait. A vain person is not liked, even if excellent in whatever he or she is doing. Arrogance, egoism and narcissism can take away grace.

The response of the observer is affected by the attitude of the performer.

Positive and negative traits

Some emotions like greed, jealousy and lust, are negative. Others, like empathy and kindness, are always desirable. However, certain traits like pride, detachment or aggressiveness, cannot be easily categorized because they are situational.

Some personal attributes can be viewed differently in terms of their intensity and extent depending on the context.

Expression is genuine, display is artificial

There is a subtle difference between expression and display of emotions. Expression of a feeling, for example love, is a reflection of what is going on inside, and is genuine. Display is contrived and artificial.

The exhibition of an emotion is merely an outward show and is different to what the person feels. With critical observation, it is possible to see through it.

We can only control our reactions

What happens in life is not always of our own choosing, but we can certainly consciously decide how we think, feel and act in response to them. There is nothing to be gained by feeling helpless or getting flustered about an unfortunate event.

Faced with an unfavorable situation, one should remain calm, think rationally and plan an appropriate course of action.

Do not push someone to the corner

In an argument or disagreement where one is proved right, allow the other person a chance to have an honorable compromise. A strategy for getting what we want is more important than the label of victory.

In a winning situation, let the other person withdraw gracefully with intact dignity.

Your attributes are not 'you'

All the characteristics we ascribe to someone - name, qualifications, occupation, status, position, personality, habits - only describe the person and do not define him. These features 'belong' to him but are not 'him' in the true sense.

One's actual identity is the soul which is eternal and beyond worldly descriptions.

Do not hesitate to change and move on

More often than not, change is for the good. However, we hesitate to leave a familiar routine because every change is initially uncomfortable. An example is when we launch into a schedule of physical exercise.

To reap the benefits of change and progress, one needs to move out of one's comfort zone and persist with the activity.

Do not crave for appreciation

Craving for recognition, adulation and acceptance is natural for a social animal like us humans. However, if this is the only source of fulfilment, it may lead to frustration.

There is nothing wrong in seeking appreciation or approval but do not be dependent on others to ratify your actions.

During a conversation note the others' reactions

When talking to someone, observe whether the person is attentive and interested in the communication. Do not presume that whatever we are saying is being received exactly as intended. The person may look bored or cynical.

In a conversation, the eyes, facial expressions and body language of the listener say it all.

Consider adversities as opportunities to improve

Do not resent adverse situations or vexing problems. They test our resilience and toughness and are opportunities to stimulate creative ideas and to search for solutions. As the saying goes, 'A smooth sea never made a skilled sailor'.

Our brain works at peak efficiency when it is presented with an issue to resolve.

Money power has limitations

Money power is often used to dominate or curb. However, one must not imagine that everyone can be influenced by this. It cannot and should not be used to control the thinking and attitude of people or force our will on the actions of others.

One must not try to manage everything with the inappropriate use of money.

Do not be too rigid with opinions

Flexibility is a virtue as long as it does not reflect fickleness. It is not a sign of weakness. Modifying a decision is appropriate and justified when there is a change in the situation or new information is available.

Ego makes us blind to changing circumstances. Do not let rigidity get in the way of rational thinking.

Make logic dominate over emotions

Whenever there is a problem or crisis one can respond with reasoning to solve the issue or succumb to emotions and take a decision based on feelings. If sentiment takes precedence over logic, planning is compromised and bias sets in.

Learn to control emotions and handle a difficult situation rationally.

Do not let others disturb the mind

We always protect our body and do not let anyone harm us physically. Similarly, we must prevent others from disturbing our mental peace and calmness and shield ourselves from provocations.

No one should be allowed to traumatize our mind and adversely affect our thoughts, feelings and mood.

Fortunate and unfortunate times keep changing

The phases of good and bad luck are episodic and transient. They follow the law of probability, and we all get a share of these. Ups and downs are a part of life.

We should enjoy the good times and successes with grace and humility, and face the misfortunes with hope, courage and submission.

Avoid giving advice to strangers

Do not meddle in the affairs of those who are not very close. We have no idea what is going on in their lives. We also do not know how our suggestions will be taken or interpreted.

Offering unsolicited advice or suggestions to unfamiliar people should be avoided. In this respect we should follow the maxim 'mind your own business'.

Do not rush to judge people

First impressions may be misleading. We often form an opinion about someone based on initial observation, but it is to be kept in mind that people do not usually reveal themselves at the outset.

An individual who appears to possess an impressive personality on first contact may turn out to be quite different as one gets to know the person better. Do not bypass the test of time!

Be aware of the peer effect

We may feel strong-willed and unaffected by what we see or hear. However, the environment and the people around us do influence the psyche.

It is best to avoid the company of deceitful people with dishonest and unprincipled practices, to prevent negativity rubbing on to you.

Perfection is the enemy of good

There are times when we should not delay a task in the pursuit of perfection. Some projects, like preparing a document, are best closed when we are satisfied that it is good enough. Otherwise, it may never see the light of day.

It is worth accepting a reasonably good product. We can go back to it later, for further improvement if necessary.

One improves by doing repeatedly

With experience one is able to perform a given task better and better. The comfort level while executing an action that has been done umpteen times, like a public speech or lecture, shows in the body language. An experienced person is relaxed and at ease, while a novice is usually stressed and anxious.

Repetition brings slow and sure improvement over a period of time.

No one likes open criticism

Criticism, especially when made in public, is resented by the recipient. Feedback is useful, but open fault-finding makes the person defensive and resistant to suggestions. It is a good idea to point out somebody's mistakes only in private.

Veiled and confidential criticism is always received better!

Spend time wisely

When we spend money, we check our resources, carefully weigh the alternatives, choose the best option, and bargain for a good deal. We do not want to waste it. We have to be even more careful while spending time.

Money may come back but time will not. Wasted time is lost forever.

You are what you think you are

As you think, so you feel. As you feel, so you do. As you do, so you are. You are the sum total of what you think. Since what you think is completely up to you, you can become as you wish to be.

If we indulge in positive, ethical, honest and progressive thoughts, we imbibe the same attributes in our character.

Handle the mind with meditation

The mind is inherently unruly and roving in nature. It has a tendency to overthink, which is an exercise in futility because it does not lead us to a resolution of any issue. Instead of trying to push the mind in one way, we can gently channelize and calm it with meditation.

Meditation is a wonderful tool to bring the mind to a desired state. Practiced effectively, it is a source of great peace and calm.

Pleasure is not the same as happiness

Pleasure is temporary and is derived from extraneous stimulation. It is addictive, leads to craving for more, and leaves a 'withdrawal' effect. Happiness, on the other hand, is a state of mind independent of external circumstances.

Pursuit of worldly pleasures actually prevents the possibility of attaining happiness!

Steps of solving a problem

Problem solving can be broken up into phases. In the first place identify, accept and recognize the problem. Then, determine the cause, consider the options for a possible solution, select the best one, and execute it.

The final stage of solving a problem is to verify that it has indeed been resolved.

Forgive but do not forget

It is natural to be upset and disturbed if anyone hurts us. How we subsequently deal with the person is important. Forgiveness relieves us of unnecessary emotional baggage, while not forgetting safeguards against repeating the mistake of relying on the person.

If someone lets you down, it is good to forgive, but wise to not forget.

Invest in quality instruments

Trying to save money and resources by choosing cheaper and less efficient devices is eventually a poor strategy. Appliances of poor quality soon become a liability and are counterproductive.

A one-time investment in equipment with sustained benefit is more fruitful than cheap high-maintenance alternatives which require frequent repair and a high running cost.

Filter the information you receive

Information overload is the result of easy access to multiple sources. We keep burdening ourselves with unnecessary details that are trivial, inconsequential, or irrelevant. It only distracts us from things that are more important and useful.

Do not let the brain be overwhelmed. Be selective about what is allowed to occupy it.

Good habits can be cultivated

If we repeat an act often enough, it becomes a routine and comes spontaneously. In order to cultivate a desirable habit, we need to consciously just keep doing it again and again.

A frequently repeated activity is eventually established at the subconscious level and becomes natural and easy.

Key periods in life need careful decisions

We can follow one routine path when everything is moving smoothly. However, when life is taking a new turn, our decisions in the face of various alternatives can take us in entirely different directions. Often, there is no possibility of return.

Extra attention is needed at the cross-roads of life. Pick the right option diligently and thoughtfully.

Do not look to others for adulation

No one is more bothered about your issues than you and your family. Your success, achievements, trophies, certificates and biodata mean little to other people. They may not view these with real happiness even if they show that they are pleased or impressed.

Go ahead and achieve, but for your own fulfilment and not for the admiration of others.

Do not let indulgence lead to dependence

Indulgence refers to pleasure and gratification through a voluntary action. Dependence on something is when you cannot do without it.

Repeated indulgence can gradually become a dependence without our realizing the transition. We can check the nature of a routine activity or habit by testing whether we can withdraw from it.

Do not misuse power

A position of power provides an opportunity to influence people and situations within one's range of control. There is a thin line between its use and abuse. One must be careful not to cross this line. It can be retained only with humility and constructive utilization.

Use of power should be restricted to positive and beneficial actions.

A leader must not be arrogant

Efficiency, foresightedness, good decision making, innovativeness, planning and problem solving ability are good leadership qualities. However, all these attributes are negated if the person exhibits arrogance.

Acceptability of a leader is greatly dependent on his or her behavior. Humility and modesty accentuate the stature.

Different problems evolve differently

There are two types of problems - those that resolve spontaneously with time, and the others which do not go away if not attended to. The former need to be left alone while the latter must be taken head on.

It is vital to differentiate between self-resolving problems and persistent or potentially escalating ones, so that the approach to handle them is appropriate.

Discussion is always better than argument

Conflicts cannot be resolved when both parties aggressively project their point of view and mentally block the other person's version. At least one side has to take the initiative to put across opinions calmly and gently.

Argument never settles a dispute. When hostility appears, logic and reason take a back seat.

Listen, do not just hear

There is a difference between listening and hearing. Mere hearing is a passive phenomenon in which the thought process is not activated. It is of no consequence since one is not likely to register it in the brain.

Listening involves understanding, interpretation and activation of a response to what is heard.

Virtues come in clusters

A good leader, colleague and family man possesses a cluster of attributes. Virtues are generally not in isolation.

A person of character has the comprehensive ability to forgive, forget, apologize, withdraw, modify, retract, adjust, empathize, appreciate, thank, facilitate and groom. It is a complete package.

Give only genuine feedback

If a friend or colleague wishes to know how he or she is performing, it is our responsibility to provide an unbiased response. There is no point in only flattering and praising if some corrections are required.

Constructive criticism can help a person to improve. Genuine and reliable feedback is much better than merely pleasing someone.

It is wise to get feedback

We all make mistakes which we may not notice. It is an unfortunate person who does not have a genuine friend or well-wisher who can point out the faults and errors.

It is smart to establish a reliable system of feedback, paving the way to corrective action.

Look at the big picture

When we are too intimately involved in an activity, we may miss keeping an eye on some vital components. Proximity can keep our attention focused on only some of the aspects.

Just as a painting is best appreciated from a little distance, it is good to step back from what one is occupied with, for a wider and more complete view.

Agree to disagree,
if there is no choice

At times people close to us may have a different view than ours on certain matters. If we thrust our opinion, it can cause unpleasantness. If one senses that the person is not willing to listen at all, it is not worth the effort.

Sometimes it is better to accept disagreement and not even try to penetrate a closed mind.

Never use harsh words

Hurtful and raucous communication is self damaging. There are occasions when we regret what we had said in the heat of the moment. We will then need to 'take our words back' because an unpleasant comment had been made based on wrong assumptions.

Keep your words soft and sweet, in case you need to eat them!

Provide critique, not criticism

There is a difference between criticism and critique. Criticism generally expresses an opinion negatively and implies finding faults with something or someone.

Critique involves an unbiased and analytic evaluation, aimed at providing feedback of positive as well as negative aspects. It gives a balanced view and conveys the true picture.

If it's important, one finds time for it.

Not having time to do a particular thing is merely an excuse. One tries to justify the failure to carry out the activity by attributing it to being too busy with other tasks.

If something is really important and essential, one will definitely find time for it. Apportionment of time is basically a matter of prioritization.

Maintain a balance in life

We need to strike a balance between work, family involvement, social interaction, maintaining health and pursuing personal passions. Every one of these aspects has its own importance. Giving disproportionate time to either of them is not right.

A successful person is one who can take care of all the facets of life with a balanced approach.

People are diverse and dissimilar

While there are many common features in human psychology, each individual brain is wired differently. Each person's nature and personality is unique. We cannot apply the experience of dealing with one person to others.

Everyone is equal but not similar. Do not interact with all the people in an identical manner and with the same expectations.

READERS NOTE

Do what would make your parents proud

There are situations when our conscience is in a dilemma about making an important decision. If one is not sure, a good way to resolve the quandary is to ask yourself whether your parents, living or otherwise, would approve of it.

Parents' instincts are the purest and they always wish "the best" for their children.

Know a person's efficiency and trustworthiness

It is good to have a dependable and loyal person working for you even if he or she is average at the job. However, development and progress is dependent on the competence and productivity of a person. We need both kinds of people in a system.

A leader should assign tasks according to the individual's efficiency and trustworthiness.

Focus on one thing at a time

Our brain can consciously pay attention to only one thing at a time. Those who claim to be capable of efficient multitasking are mistaken.

When we try to attend to multiple things together, except reflex or purely mechanical actions, we actually rapidly keep shifting focus between them. The need for repeated reorientation decreases efficiency and output in each of the tasks.

A sufferer needs help, not just compassion

Sympathy, empathy and compassion represent an increasing level of understanding of another person's suffering and the inclination to do something about it.

It is not enough to just feel sorry for someone in distress. Our real contribution is when we not only recognize the feelings of the person but also take positive steps to help out.

The surroundings resonate with the mind

Our mind vibrates at a certain frequency. Our surroundings pick up these energies and the environment resonates similarly. If we modify our thoughts and feelings, our actions change and that affects the atmosphere around us.

Think positive and things around will also turn positive.

Some things remain in memory without conscious effort

We can remember details of things by deliberating on what we have learnt. However, physical skills like riding a cycle or swimming are acquired by sheer repetition and are reflexly recalled. These simple acts are not driven by thought.

Memory is processed at a conscious or subconscious level, and different activities need dissimilar type of recall.

Performance is driven by the mind

Our thought process influences and directs our actions. A defeatist attitude retards meaningful effort that is required to succeed. Lack of conviction acts like a brake and paralyses the person.

Don't imagine failure even before trying. Be confident and one will certainly perform better.

Believe in your ability

Hope and conviction are the fuels of activity. Success is preceded by focused and intense effort, which in turn is a result of belief in our ability to accomplish a feat. Amazing achievement is possible if we trust ourselves.

We can if we think we can.

Avoid getting angry

Anger is an enemy of peace and happiness. Develop patience, acceptance and self-control to avoid getting angry. Control the initial negative ripples of vexation in the mind and nip it in the bud.

Anger always leaves a distraught and disturbed feeling; then why let it happen to yourself!

Don't believe everything - you see or hear.

What we hear and see may be just an illusion and not necessarily the truth. Perceptions must not be assumed to be a reality. Appearances can be deceptive. The saying 'there is more to it than meets the eye' suggests that one may be misled by some observations. Hearsay should be taken with a grain of salt.

Conclusions must not be drawn without verifying the authenticity and genuineness.

Know your body!

Everyone is different. One may be blessed with fitness, strength, flexibility and strong immunity. Conversely, there may be specific allergies, predispositions and sensitivities. We may suffer from certain ailments and infirmities.

We should know our body so that we can take positive advantage of its strengths and protect its weaknesses.

Have right duration of sleep

How much sleep does one need? It is indicated by the feeling of freshness and energy when one wakes up. Studies suggest that 6 to 7 hours are optimum. The need varies with the physical and mental state while one is awake. Lethargy and listlessness on waking imply too little or too much sleep.

Make sure you get the right amount of sleep to feel fresh and rejuvenated.

Removing the negative, results in the positive

Negative and positive things cannot exist together. Removing negative emotions like anger, resentment, worry, regret, guilt, jealousy, blame, greed and arrogance leave the mind in a positive state.

By simply getting rid of undesirable feelings, one finds that good ones gradually take over.

A precedent does not justify a wrong act

People sometimes quote a precedent to justify an action which someone got away with, in spite of being ethically or legally incorrect. A bad example should not be used to defend or validate a thing that lacks merit.

If a wrongdoing has gone unnoticed or unpunished, it does not mean that it can be repeated.

Whatever is successful will be repeated

Any act, good or bad, is bound to be repeated if it 'works'. Appreciating and rewarding a good feat is an effective method to ensure that it will be done again. On the other hand, if a child gets away with a little lie or a trivial theft, he or she gets the confidence to do it again.

It is important to ensure that only good actions are allowed to succeed while negative deeds are nipped in the bud.

To be happy, make others happy

Those who think they can attain happiness at the cost of other people are sadly mistaken. We cannot fill ourselves with joy by making others unhappy and miserable. Only a sadist derives pleasure from causing sorrow or pain.

The most effective way to be happy is to bring smiles and laughter in the lives of those around.

Assign specific responsibilities in a team

As a leader of a team engaged in a project that is beyond the capacity of a single person, optimum assignment of individual roles is important. Allocating responsibility of distinct components to each team member produces best results.

Specific responsibility facilitates dedicated effort and accountability.

Have faith, everything happens for some good!

We often get disturbed by some adverse events affecting us. Pre-judgement of apparently negative situations or setbacks shows our ignorance of the grand scheme God has cut out for us.

We must remain grateful for all the blessings and face difficult situations with faith and courage.

How to be a likeable person

Everyone wants to be liked by others. However, a grouchy, stiff, unapproachable, ill-behaved and nasty person will never be popular even if one is talented and intelligent.

We can expect to be adulated and admired only if we have a pleasant, cordial, well-mannered, supportive and compassionate nature.

Nothing is permanent

Nothing in this world is everlasting or eternal. This realization is unnerving and reassuring at the same time. We tend to get disappointed when good times come to an end, but so do bad ones. Acceptance of the temporary and transient nature of everything provides peace and serenity.

All that happens in life needs to be taken in one's stride.

Practice yoga and meditation for a balanced life

The time-tested approach to maintain a fit body and mind is to have a balanced lifestyle which includes a daily routine of meditation and yoga. Yoga is not just about postures and stretches. It is a complete way of life and involves adopting the proper way to breathe, eat, exercise and think.

Meditation helps us to maintain mental balance.

Good habits may need to be imposed

Parents and teachers often need to enforce some unpleasant routines on children in order to inculcate good habits. Simple tasks like making the bed, keeping the room clean or maintaining a time schedule are initially detested and resisted by kids.

Gradually, the regularly carried out activities become ingrained and are no longer disliked or avoided.

Calm the mind before falling asleep

The moments before we slip into sleep determine how we will feel on awakening. The state of mind before falling asleep affects the quality of sleep and is retained over its entire duration. If we are disturbed or upset as we lie down on the bed, sleep does not seem to refresh us.

Bringing oneself to a state of calmness through quiet reflection or prayer while going to bed enhances the relaxing effect of sleep.

Learn to listen and listen to learn

When we speak, it is only a communication of what we already know. However, when we listen, something new is always learnt since it is akin to peeping into someone's mind carrying its own knowledge, experience and thought process.

Listening attentively is a great source of learning.

Think before you speak

The more we speak, the more likely we are to say something which need not or should not have been uttered. Spoken words cannot be taken back. Many interpersonal conflicts are aggravated by unnecessarily talking too much without weighing the words.

Especially in delicate situations, think carefully before saying anything so that it is not regretted later.

Good communication improves relationships

Most interpersonal problems are a result of imperfect communication. We cannot read others' mind. Wrong conclusions are drawn through assumptions if one's thoughts are not effectively conveyed.

Misunderstanding and mistrust among friends, colleagues and family members can be prevented by communicating properly.

Convince, don't coerce.

If we try to enforce orders on people working with us, they may not openly defy or refuse to obey, but efficiency is compromised. Creation of interest, encouragement and gentle persuasion produce better results. A congenial environment improves output.

Imposition begets resistance and is counter-productive.

How one treats less privileged reveals character

If we want to judge the true character of someone with power, we need to just observe how the person deals with less privileged people on whom there is no dependence for anything. Is he or she gentle, kind, tolerant, compassionate and supportive?

Exhibition of power with arrogance and haughtiness are despicable.

Verify information before believing it

On receiving a piece of information, one should not jump to conclusions without verifying its authenticity and genuineness. Checking the source and its reliability is critical before forming any impression or opinion.

Everything we hear or read may not necessarily be true and could have been circulated with a motive.

Gratitude is unconditional

When someone offers a gift in return for a service, how does one make out whether it is out of gratefulness or is a bribe? If it is extended even before the job has been completed, or the person needs further favors in the future, it is likely to be just a form of inducement.

Gratitude is unconditional thankfulness with no further expectations or demands.

Principles of medical ethics also apply to life

The four principles in Medicine are Autonomy, Beneficence, Nonmaleficence and Justice. These indicate that the right to choose treatment rests with the patients, doctors must always do good to them, never do any harm and treat all patients alike respectively.

As in Medicine, in everyday life each person should decide for himself, do good to others, never harm anybody and treat everyone with respect.

A person is more than the title

How we should deal with someone does not depend only on the position or status. Our approach needs to be adapted to the nature, temperament and character of the person. For this, keen observation is required to determine what kind of individual he or she is.

There are many facets of a person's personality.

Give the most important work to the best person

While distributing tasks, it is prudent to delegate the important ones to the best worker and leave the rest for others. Do not burden the most talented person with mundane work that anyone can carry out. Use the skills for things others cannot do well.

Utilizing the service of the most skillful person optimally is itself a skill.

All relationships need time and attention

Relationships are built over time with emotions, care and application. We cannot leave them unattended. Like plants, they need to be constantly nurtured and groomed.

Never take relationships with nears and dears for granted. It can get spoiled without our realizing it, if we do not pay attention.

Non-verbal signs tell the real story

Body language, spontaneous actions and tone of voice convey a lot about what somebody is thinking and feeling, if one is really observant. In fact, people may not be conscious that these clues are being communicated to those around them.

We can choose and control what we speak, but involuntary non-verbal clues give us away.

An open mind is needed for progress

Moving forward necessitates exposure to new situations and experiences. We should be ready to consider and use fresh and untested strategies with an open mind. How will we know whether something works or not, without trying it out?

Progress entails being receptive to different ideas and opinions.

Real achievement is the respect earned

The most meaningful achievement is not one's designation, financial status, wide recognition, awards received or an impressive biodata. These become irrelevant if the person is not liked by the people around.

A successful person is a real winner if he or she has earned the respect and adulation of colleagues and subordinates as well.

How to bring out the best in others

Different skills are required to get the best outcomes from children, subordinates and colleagues. No single strategy works for all. One needs to use authority, coercion, guidance and supervision, whichever is best suited for the person.

People work best when they feel comfortable and motivated. A gentle approach, trust, encouragement and appreciation are the best tools to bring out the best.

Hold back the impulsive response

In tense moments of anger or hurt, it is common to exhibit a negative behavior which one may regret later. Deliberately holding back, the impulse for even a few seconds can save us from saying or doing something that cannot be reversed.

Do not react immediately to a provocative situation. The responses are always more logical when one waits for some time before responding.

Do not compare yourself with anyone

Comparison is the root cause of misery. No two people have identical assets or belongings. The moment one starts comparing oneself with others it generates an inferiority complex, jealousy and consequently lack of self-respect and confidence.

Count the many blessings bestowed by the almighty which others do not have, and let gratitude fill the heart.

Dealing with unreasonable directions

If an authority gives an instruction or direction that makes us uncomfortable since it is not right and ethical, it is better to discuss it. Give your opinion rather than regretting it and feeling guilty after having done it hesitantly.

When one discusses logically and respectfully the senior will mostly understand and agree with the right path.

People work harder if their contribution is recognized

When many members of a team are engaged in a work, the total output is usually more than when each person works separately. Collective work is more productive. However, people do it individually since they feel their contribution might not get due recognition.

It would be best if we could make sure that the contribution of each member in a team gets quantified.

Allocate specific tasks to team members

When we give a task to a group of people, it must be made sure that each person is involved with a specific, identifiable component that can be observed and measured. This prevents unnecessary duplication of work and enables monitoring of individual performance.

A team achieves the best results when each member knows the value of their own contribution.

Weigh the pros and cons before an irreversible action

Before taking an irretrievable step, the benefits and harms, the pros and cons should be considered. For very significant decisions it is always good to be aware of the consequences before taking the final step.

The time spent on pre-assessment is always good, so that we do not repent later for something that we cannot redo or change.

Skills acquired in childhood do not go waste

Good habits picked up in childhood give an advantage throughout life. Activities like reading books, drawing, participation in sports, public speaking, good handwriting, learning about gadgets and solving puzzles should be encouraged.

Skills learnt as a child may start as a hobby but often translate into an asset in one's profession and career.

Strive for better communication and interaction

Interpersonal relationships can suffer when two minds do not meet and interact. Misunderstanding, misinterpretation and mistrust can be removed by exchange of thoughts and ideas.

Mutual respect and love stems from free and frank communication, and vice versa.

It is good to be able to forget

A sound memory is surely an asset. However, the ability to forget some things is a blessing sometimes. Keeping unnecessary, useless, disturbing and negative thoughts in mind can be troublesome. Getting rid of these can bring peace and serenity.

Forget things which are not worth remembering.

Fire in the belly!

An intense desire to succeed will always generate the required actions and efforts till the goal is attained. How badly we long for something determines how hard we will try to achieve it. The obstacles and problems in the path will not stop us from moving forward.

As they say, "If the desire is intense, the entire universe helps and even conspires for our success".

Healthy competition is always good

Competing with others and scoring over them may be a necessity in many situations. However, it should not generate hostility, jealousy and schadenfreude. In fact, mostly one should focus on trying to do the best and not be distracted by others.

Use competition as a reason for self-improvement.

Compete with 'self only'

The only person we should compete with is our own self. Set appropriate and feasible goals and keep on inspiring yourself with positive instincts. Gradual improvement is bound to occur, and amazing things will happen.

Aim and work towards becoming a better and more capable person every day.

Basic nature does not change

A zebra, as they say, does not change its stripes. If a person has betrayed once, he or she can do it again. Forgiveness after an apology is all fine, but trusting again in the future can result in another betrayal!

A person's character does not easily change. Do not expect a cheater to turn over a new leaf. Well, everyone may not agree with this opinion.

Every skill has an application

No skill is wasted. If we are very good at something, it is important to just focus on developing it to the best extent possible. How we will be able to utilize the exceptional talent may not be immediately obvious.

We discover suitable applications of special abilities, as appropriate situations emerge.

Ability is a gift of God

It is natural to feel proud when one achieves something, but it must be kept in mind that the skill which enabled the success has actually been bestowed by God. Do not allow vanity and ego to disregard this truth.

One can do nothing without the blessings of the Almighty. Always stay grateful.

Like the body, the tired brain needs a break

While working continuously, one often fails to realize that our brain is like an electric battery needing to be periodically charged. Performance is linked with a high energy level which needs to be maintained.

To maintain efficiency and a clear mind, a 'detox' break with relaxation and rest is essential.

The first creative product is often the best

If one wants to sample the writings of an author who has penned several books, it is a good idea to choose the first one. This is the one in which the writer has put the heart and soul and felt most strongly about.

The quality of an original work is of course proportional to the time, focus and effort put into it.

Setbacks teach us more

A problem, obstacle or complication is not just a bad situation, it is also an opportunity to learn. It shakes off complacency, forces us to address important issues, and teaches us how to face such circumstances in the future.

Do not grudge and lament while facing difficult conditions.

Negate negative thoughts

Our natural and default state is peace and calm. Negative thoughts like hate, anger, ego and jealousy pull us down, spoil the mood and make us sad or irritated. If we can eliminate such feelings, we would remain much happier.

Avoiding or getting rid of negatives leaves a positive state.

A small extra effort can bring much better results

The time and energy spent in doing any work with full dedication and commitment is not much more than that in merely going through the motions, but the results do improve considerably. Putting in your best effort is worth it.

A little additional input pays rich dividends!

Communication is the key

Interpersonal relationships often suffer when two minds do not meet, even when the hearts do. Communication helps to allay doubts and misunderstandings. It shows the other person's love and concern. These cannot be taken for granted and need to be expressed.

Keeping communication open helps to maintain a healthy connection.

Hesitation to interact is a missed opportunity

Many times, we hesitate to initiate a conversation, introduce ourselves and express our views with someone new. We may keep waiting in vain for an appropriate time and end up regretting it later.

If the other person also avoids taking the initiative, one will miss an opportunity of having a fruitful interaction and even the beginning of a long friendship!

It is natural to have difference of opinion

There is no opinion in the world that has no counter-opinion. If we keep an open mind, we may be able to understand the other person's perspective that justifies the thinking. Difference of opinion can either be resolved by discussion or by gracefully accepting it without prejudice.

All individuals are entitled to have their point of view.

READERS NOTE

Be flexible

Acknowledge possibilities instead of having a rigid viewpoint on any matter. No one can be absolutely right all the time. It is wise to allow the mind to accept thoughts of 'it may be so' as well as 'it is not necessarily so'.

Being flexible is a significant part of being rational.

Value the soul in the body

The body is visible and always gets preference and precedence in self-care and in forming an opinion about others. The soul within determines the true self of the person. We must spend time and thoughts on the soul to be at peace and also to judge others.

The body is temporary. The soul is eternal.

Learn strategies for improving memory

Attention, association and repetition are the key determinants of a good memory. Apply focus and concentration on what you want to learn, relate the content to things already known using as much imagery as possible, and repeat this process frequently.

One can use these simple ways to remember and recall things better.

The more we give the richer we are

Richness and poverty are relative terms. Worth is determined not by what we have but by what we have to offer. Poor and unfortunate is the person who owns a fortune but will not share it. The other way round is also true. This applies to finances, knowledge, skills and wisdom.

If one cannot give, it is of no use!

Try to acquire needs, not wants

When we feel like acquiring or owning something, we should ask ourselves whether it is needed or just wanted. Needs are limited and fulfilling them is gratifying. On the other hand, wants tend to be progressively extravagant and insatiable.

Aim to satisfy the needs. Everything else is unnecessary.

A risk may or may not be worth taking

Always think before taking a risk, as to whether it is worth taking or not. Weigh the value, necessity, justification and the likely benefits of the action against the probability of failure and level of the loss. The risk of doing nothing might be more than the risk of active intervention.

Go ahead and take a risk, if the anticipated benefit is more than the potential harm.

Do not take things for granted

Nothing can be taken for granted. A sudden illness, an accident or a stroke of bad luck can change the entire picture of life. Just revel in the present and be thankful when things go well, but don't be surprised or rattled by adverse happenings.

Never assume that everything will happen as one plans or expects.

This too will pass!

Everything in this world is transient. Do not despair misfortunes. Bad times do not last, and for that matter nor do good times. Just enjoy the moments and don't wait for special events or occasions. They would also not remain for long anyway.

Sooner or later, all things have to come to an end.

An opinion is not necessarily an advice

Advice is valuable if it provides some added information or insight that one did not know or had considered. It is given with a definitive direction. Hence, one can use it in making the right decision. Opinions are expressed as thoughts one has on the aspect, with an open mind.

Advice is actionable, opinion is just someone's viewpoint.

Correctness should get precedence over being right

There is a subtle difference between being 'right' and being 'correct'. One may well have justification to defend an action as technically right but if it is not a reasonable and sensible decision it would not be correct in a particular situation and should rather not be done.

Taking a wise step is better than doing something that may appear to be right but is inappropriate under the given circumstances.

The worst fears we have, actually never happen

Unfounded fears can often disturb our mental peace. There is only a remote possibility that what we dread will actually happen. Curb the negative thoughts and baseless imagination and think of the more likely and logical outcomes.

Exaggerated dangers and perils that lurk in the mind and haunt us, seldom materialize.

Arrogance tarnishes the charm of brilliance

Expertise and brilliance in work can get negated when there is arrogance and snobbish behavior with colleagues and subordinates. Such a person is disliked in spite of the achievements and is likely to face rejection and failure in the long run.

There is nothing better than excellence coupled with decency.

Unused resources soon get depleted

Anything that is meant to be used will deteriorate, decay or devalue if left unutilized. The adage 'use it or lose it' applies not only to machines, money or time, but also to our physical body and mental skills.

It is not what we have but what we do with it that matters.

Step wise approach to getting work done

A good leader should look at various aspects, in order to get the best out of subordinates. Firstly, allocate a specific and doable task to each individual depending on their capabilities and skills. Secondly, give a time limit. Third and most importantly, give due credit to each one when the job finishes. It is a motivating factor for the future.

Getting work done is an art which can be learnt.

An angry person is actually afraid

Anger and fear have the same physiological origin. Both are a natural fight / flight response to an acute overwhelming situation. Once we comprehend this phenomenon, we would approach an angry individual with a bit more sympathy and understanding.

A person who is angry is just reacting aggressively to something he or she cannot handle rationally.

Modern day stress rarely needs a 'fight or flight' response

We are no longer living in a jungle where a fight or flight reaction was required for sudden life-threatening physical dangers. Such dire circumstances rarely appear in modern life. Stress is mostly mental now a days and such physical reactions are not justified!

A calm mind and a measured response are required in most stressful situations.

Be aware and conscious of the learning curve

There is a learning curve and time frame for mastering a new skill. This is largely similar in all of us. The initial period requires careful planning and full concentration. As one performs the act repeatedly, it becomes easier and easier.

There are no short cuts to expertise and excellence. Enjoy the process and do not take the journey with stress.

Have no ego in seeking advice

We should always be open to seeking advice from a person having more experience and knowledge. It should be someone who can be trusted for a sincere and unbiased opinion. We will surely get some simple and useful tips. As they say, we do not have to commit every mistake ourselves.

Wise counsel helps to think differently and better. Of course, the final decision is kept with oneself only.

Always be kind and compassionate

Compassion is a way of thinking and a characteristic of a person. A humane person will be considerate and benevolent to all living creatures. Be kind to all but especially to the deprived and vulnerable, irrespective of caste, race or religion.

Kind people have less ego and are not greedy or self-centered. They are also spiritually elevated.

Handle difficult situations rationally

Problems and difficult situations are bound to come in life. Keep calm, assess the severity and implications of the issue, and consider the plausible options rationally without undue emotion and haste.

We usually do find a satisfactory solution to any problem when it is faced with adequate focus, application and a positive attitude.

Do good without any expectations

When we do something for a colleague, friend or subordinate, it should be an unconditional act. Never do it as a favor and have no expectations in return. This will help create a strong relationship and will give immense satisfaction which is enough of a return.

Do good to others and do not dwell on it.

Keep it simple and just do it

Some important things that we want to do 'very well' get delayed so much at times that they lose their value or get missed altogether. This could be related to a variety of activities like organizing a program, writing a report or article, starting a project or visiting some place.

When you plan any activity, make up your mind firmly and just do it without waiting endlessly for perfection.

Ponder on what you call a 'successful life'

Success in life is not just about designations, positions, awards or bank balance. Of course, these credentials are typically linked to the definition of success but ultimately it is happiness, satisfaction and being respected that are more important.

A person with a happy family life, good relationships and work ethics who may be less decorated is definitely more successful.

Stay with good people

It is impossible not to be affected or influenced by the company one keeps. Avoid pessimistic, abusive and unethical people. They will only create an unpleasant and stressful environment and will pass on negative vibes.

Life is happier and more gratifying if one is among virtuous people with a positive attitude and good moral values.

Divide work, according to aptitude

Within an organization or a family, it is a good idea to divide the work among each other depending on the skills and aptitude of the individuals. Duplication is thereby avoided, and each person can focus on whatever he or she is good at.

With the best contribution of each of the members of a team, the output is optimized.

Develop a team

Developing a team and distributing work promotes synergy and increases output. Each person becomes more proficient by focusing on his or her part, and repetition of the task improves efficiency.

A good leader is one who tactfully allocates responsibilities according to each individual's attitude, education, skill and capability.

Be fair to yourself

In life we may have to face setbacks due to many extraneous factors. Never let them affect you and do not blame yourself. One can only do his or her best with commitment, honesty and sincerity, leaving the result to destiny.

Just keep moving on your path with confidence and self-respect. Success will come sooner or later.

Different people have different skills

No two individuals have the same abilities and competence. As a leader, one should not handle or deal with all the subordinates in an identical manner. The skill lies in identifying and utilizing their specific qualities.

Individualize the interaction with each team member, so that the best can be brought out of them while maintaining a good relationship.

Lead a balanced life

Focusing only on work and skill development is likely to compromise social life and relationships. Conversely, spending too much time on entertainment at the cost of further learning can prevent progress in the profession.

We have to strike a healthy balance between work, family, friends and enjoyment.

Know the recipe for professional success

To do well at the workplace, one needs sound academic knowledge, good hand skills, ability to acquire new things, persistence, communication skills, good record keeping and the ability to project one's abilities. Company of brilliant people, team spirit and healthy competition also contribute.

A combination of several attributes is required for success in the profession.

Self-respect is vital

Respect for one's own self is a prerequisite to having confidence and an impressive personality. While narcissism and excessive self-worth or ego is bad and eventually harms, positive regard for self is a good attribute.

Self-esteem is reflected socially as well as professionally. It determines how we project ourselves and how others perceive us.

READERS NOTE

Be respectful to others

Respect and disrespect are generally reciprocated. If we are disrespectful, others will have contempt for us. Of course, some people may remain polite since that is their nature, or they may not be in a position to show their true feelings.

If we want people to have respect for us, we have to show them the same courtesy.

Have a 'we' approach to life

Some people always think and talk in terms of 'I' and are primarily concerned only with themselves. Persons with a 'we' approach to life have good rapport with friends and colleagues with genuine warmth and caring. They are compassionate and cooperative.

Those who are good at sharing joys and sorrows are always liked and sought after.

Discuss issues, not individuals

In conversations with friends, colleagues and family members, we should discuss issues, ideas and positive strategies instead of individuals. Chatting about particular persons tends to drift into meaningless gossip and is of no benefit to anyone.

Time spent on purposeful and educative discussion pays dividends.

Do not carry the work stresses to home

After the day's work, the pressures and stresses of one's job should not be carried home. It will help to relax and be ready for the next day. Similarly, do not allow home issues to affect performance at the workplace.

We should not spoil family time with problems related to our professional occupation.

Replace the vices with virtues

The 'seven great vices' are best avoided or removed by inculcating the corresponding virtues. Move from anger to patience, pride to humility, lust to chastity, greed to charity, gluttony to temperance, envy to gratitude and sloth to diligence.

Vices and virtues are mutually exclusive and cannot exist together. Choose the virtues.

Get familiar with gadgets

Many new gadgets keep appearing in the workplace and at home. The sooner one gets familiar with them the better. Study the catalogue, learn the applications and spend time playing with the buttons.

Avoidance or hesitation in accepting new devices will not help since they have become part of our life now.

Coping with stress

The 'triple A' strategy of alter/avoid/accept is the best way to deal with whatever is creating stress. Firstly, try to 'alter' the situation or mend the individual causing it. In case that is not possible, attempt to 'avoid' the situation or the concerned person.

If one cannot remove or keep away from the source of stress, it is best to 'accept' it and move on in life.

The right way to lose weight

Some people attempt to slim down by vigorous exercise without adjusting their food habits. Others try to starve themselves but remain inactive. Both methods are unhealthy and ineffective.

To reduce weight, regular walk/exercise as well as balanced diet are equally important.

Beware of the universal vices

All religions teach us to shun anger, hatred, greed, ego and jealousy. Excessive attachment and craving for worldly attractions is also bad. We should make a conscious effort to avoid these, since they slowly and repeatedly tend to creep in.

A periodic self-check is useful to stay away from the wrongs which are universally identified.

Do not lose the long-term perspective

Sometimes problems of immediate concern consume us so much that we are left with no time for things that may not be urgent but are essential. Those issues may actually be much more relevant in the future.

Do not get lost in day-to-day matters and keep attending to affairs with long-term importance also.

Trust the experts

Once we have chosen a consultant, whether a doctor, lawyer, architect, chartered accountant, dietitian or a physiotherapist, we must have faith in the person. Do not carry doubts or interfere in the professional planning and execution.

Have faith in the experts and follow their advice when you seek help. Of course, your knowledge of the subject will help you execute it better.

Beware of the oversweet as well as the hypercritical

Before taking praise or criticism too seriously, keep in mind what kind of person it is coming from. Some people have a habit of praising everything; enjoy it but do not be overly elated. Others are always critical; listen but do not get upset.

Do not be unduly affected by such overly expressive people.

Have a role model

Whichever profession one is in, it is good to have one or two role models. People who are successful and respected are so for a reason. They always have some qualities which are worth understanding and emulating.

One can learn a lot by just watching accomplished people and trying to follow their ways.

Real success is never a flash in the pan

Many times, when we see a successful person, we think that they have just been fortunate. Their hard work, dedication and struggle may not be known to us. Of course, good luck is important, but there are no short cuts.

It may not be realized that most achievers have been through long periods of planning, preparation, problem solving and then proper execution.

Make gradual change

As a leader in an organization, at home and even within own self, one may feel a need for change in the functioning and systems. Always make it gradual and unhurried. Rapid shifts can create undue disturbance and disruption.

The effects of measured change will unfold slowly, and one can revert if no benefits are noted, or unforeseen complications arise.

Experience can change beliefs

We often have strong beliefs and convictions about a variety of issues. As we gain experience, we realize that some of our earlier opinions turned out to be wrong. This should have a humbling effect and make us less opinionated.

We should be careful not to form rigid views about things which we cannot possibly know everything about.

Specific expertise versus multiple skills

Small workplace setups usually require multitasking. Places with several professionals working together need individuals with specific expertise. At times we might have an option to decide our role.

The situation at the place of work will determine whether it is required to master one skill or to perform multiple tasks, and one needs to adapt accordingly.

Be prepared for adversities in life

Life, as they say, is not a bed of roses. Things may unfold in an unpredictable manner, and the results of our actions may be quite different to what we expect or anticipate.

One needs to be prepared for unexpected twists and turns in events and adapt accordingly. Taking things for granted can result in disappointment and failure.

Staying on top needs skill

Reaching the top and staying there needs different skills. One may acquire a position through talent and sheer hard work, but how long one is able to maintain that status depends more on soft skills.

Strict discipline, continuous effort, positive attitude and good interpersonal relationships are all required to stay on top once success is attained.

Life follows the law of probability

Things cannot be accurately predicted and only their likelihood can be estimated. The relative chance of a specific occurrence may vary. We can observe trends and gauge the probability of certain outcomes, but nothing is an absolute certainty.

Anything is possible in life, and we can be taken by surprise. Learn to accept the unexpected.

Accept what is beyond control

We cannot direct all the external events and happenings, but the way we think about them is in our power. Since they are not within our control, there is no point in being unduly affected. Acceptance is the only option.

The realization that something is beyond one's control can itself be a source of peace and tranquility.

How one would want to be remembered!

We all have to go one day, and only our memories will remain. Consider whether the best tag would be that of a successful dynamic achiever, a rich famous figure, an intellectual or that of an excellent human being.

Surely one would want to be remembered as a person with a heart of gold, full of love and compassion.

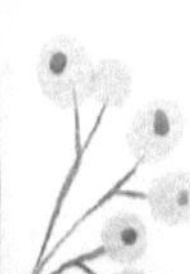

One cannot know everything

Brilliant young people often have the illusion of being pretty 'enlightened' and that they 'know everything'. As we mature, experience makes it clear that we are all just scratching the surface of knowledge. Hopefully, humility then sets in.

Acknowledgement that one actually knows very little is the first step to learning.

Smile and laugh to feel better

We wear our emotions on our faces. Facial expression spontaneously reflects the inner feelings. Intriguingly, it works the other way round too. If we deliberately alter our countenance, it can change how we are feeling.

Make a conscious effort to change the facial expression when feeling sad, by switching to a smile, and notice that the mood changes for the better.

Do not magnify minor problems

Sometimes we let trivial issues unduly disturb us. Learn to handle small irritants and do not let them affect the mood. It is later realized that we ruined our day over a matter that had no long-term implications.

Do not dwell on minor problems and failures. Little setbacks should not be allowed to overwhelm us.

Enjoy your work

The most important aspect of success at a job is that we should be completely dedicated and passionate about what we are doing. Unless pleasure is being derived while performing the duties, we will not put in our best effort.

All the abilities and skills collectively cannot produce the desired results if one is not enjoying the work.

Do not rush to act on a problem

Faced with a problem, the initial reaction is to solve it immediately. However, with a rash approach the outcome is not likely to be the best one. Unless it is urgent, it is better to 'incubate' a vexatious issue in the mind.

In a difficult situation, let the thoughts churn for as long as appropriate and feasible. Usually, the best solution consolidates and becomes clear.

Channelize the mind

If we do not control the mind, it can wander about, create confusion, generate worry and anxiety, and indulge in negativity. However, when we channelize thinking, it becomes clear and constructive.

Keep the mind on a positive track at all times.

Do not wait for symptoms to appear

Some common non-communicable diseases do not cause symptoms for a long time but silently damage the body. One in three adults have high blood pressure and one in eight have diabetes. Similarly high cholesterol levels are without symptoms.

Do not presume to be healthy, if you do not feel unwell. Periodic checkup and testing help in early detection.

Simplify things for others to follow

Skill, effort and wisdom is required to simplify a complex and complicated system or process. It then becomes easier to grasp and follow, whether it is a lecture, book, guideline, instruction or procedure.

Clarity and ease in understanding any mode of communication helps in better acceptability and greater use by everyone.

Do not give advice unless it is asked for

Never give unsolicited or unwanted advice to anyone. At times it may generate a feeling of imposition or intrusion into the privacy of others.

If one does offer counsel to someone, the attitude and response during the process should be closely observed. In case the person is not listening attentively or shows disinterest, one might as well stop.

All religions teach us love and compassion

There is hardly any difference in the teachings of the holy books of various religions. All preach love and compassion. Sadly, some self-styled so called custodians of religion distort the messages of the scriptures and promote divisiveness, even hatred.

We should stick to the original verses and teachings of sages.

Analyze and then respond

Do not pass judgement on or reject a new thing straight away. There is a natural tendency to resist change. As the implications are analyzed, we may reach the conclusion that it is for the betterment.

A change is always uncomfortable and sometimes threatening, but it often brings improvement if it has been well thought out.

Take advantage of a 'boring' day

Sometimes we feel that we are having a boring day. In fact, we should thank God for it. It means that nothing untoward is happening. Such moments are obviously calm and are best for mental and physical rejuvenation.

On quiet days one gets time to be with self, think positively, do exercise and follow a hobby.

Seek guidance wherever necessary

Students generally take advice from seniors and teachers while learning academic subjects like physics, math and science. In life, it is equally helpful to seek guidance from a wise person while searching for abstract goals like happiness, peace and contentment.

A dependable and learned guide is very useful facilitator to put us on the right track.

Keep thinking of alternatives

As a part of an organization, we become so used to following instructions that we may stop using our imagination. Of course, the treaded ways and established protocols are generally good and time-tested, but options are always there.

If one keeps on thinking of better alternatives, more efficient ways of doing something will surely be found.

Acknowledge the generation gap

The world changes significantly every few years. The norms and ways of the new generation are different from the previous. One should keep this phenomenon in mind and accept it graciously.

Life becomes easier and more comfortable when one recognizes and understands that change is the only constant in life.

Note down things to remember

We are so busy with day-to-day activities that we may at times forget some important dates and tasks. It is a good habit to note down things to do and dates to remember, regarding occasions and deadlines. We will not have to repent or regret later, if we make it a habit.

It is very satisfying to make use of a 'reminder' file and strike the items off the list as they are completed.

Be gentle while correcting someone

While pointing out someone's mistake, if we angrily reprimand the person he or she gets upset, feels insulted, withdraws and is not able to bring about the desired change. On the other hand, gently making the individual understand what is wrong and how to improve usually helps the cause.

When we lose temper, the whole purpose is lost in the communication process

Mental strength is more important than physical

Physical and mental health do go side by side, but lack of confidence and resolve are major handicaps even if one is physically strong. On the contrary, many people with some physical limitations are mentally so tough that they do not let the constraint affect their capacity.

'Will power' is the strongest power!

Aspire for just enough

Happiness and peace of mind have nothing to do with abundance of money, possessions, fame or status. Of course, a lack of them can be a source of distress, but there is a level of each which is adequate for comfortable living.

Running after material gains can be an endless pursuit. Have satiety and control over desires.

Do not be too attached

People who have an insatiable desire for possessions and material things accumulate much more than they actually need. They are scared of losing what they own and are always under stress.

One should enjoy what one has but must not be too attached to or obsessed with it. Learn to take losses and damages in stride.

Do not try to succeed by unfair means

When youngsters see a person gaining prosperity and fame despite breaking rules and ethical principles, they may get attracted to those ways. They need to be told that such so-called 'success' is farcical and transient. Truth eventually catches up and fake success does not last long.

Success through actual class and caliber might be slow to come but is surely sustained.

Enjoy the journey, not just the destination

The process of an educational activity or learning of an art or procedure is to be relished. Even if we do not eventually reach the goal, some skills would have been acquired and some lessons learnt.

If one is obsessed with just the final outcome of an activity, the experience is made less pleasurable. After all, life itself is a journey which is to be enjoyed.

Avoid arguments on religion and politics

People generally have clear and strong views on politics and religion. Instead of trying to convince anyone to change their opinion on such matters, it is better to discuss other topics like health, science, art, literature and philosophy.

Arguments on sensitive issues which are personal and close to one's heart only spoil relationships.

The healthy food diary

A good daily menu is rich in fresh seasonal fruits and vegetables, high fiber whole grains, nuts, low fat dairy products, high protein plants like legumes, pulses, soya products and quinoa, as well as animal protein sources like lean meat and sea foods.

For a healthy diet, cut down on salt, trans fats, saturated fat, high sugar beverages, red meat, egg yolk and preserved foods.

Avoid talking just about yourself

One should avoid too much of 'I, me, my' in conversation. The matter might be our top priority but not necessarily so for others. It is better to use more of 'we, our' if not 'you, your'. Excessive expression of what you think, what you did and who you are, puts off people.

Talk about yourself only if someone asks a direct question.

Express your opinion but do not rub it in

It is good to express an opinion when one is convinced about something. The problem arises when one aggressively justifies it and tries to make others agree to it. It can become an argument and result in an unnecessary and unpleasant situation.

We cannot forcibly change the thoughts of people and should not even have the desire to do it.

It is easier to acquire skills in childhood

Childhood is the most effective time to acquire a skill. If parents guide their children and provide opportunities to pick up special abilities early, it requires less effort. They can then sharpen and use the prowess as they grow.

One can learn new things at any age, but it is more difficult and time-consuming in adults as compared to children.

Enjoyment and success at work go hand in hand

Some people love their work, some do it as a duty, and some hate the work thrust upon them. Enjoying what we do always leads to better efficiency and output. Improved results and outcome then itself become a source of pleasure.

If we love our work, we will enjoy doing it and the results will always be positive.

Be conscious of God all the time

Rather than remembering God only when we are in a crisis or have something to ask for, we should think of the Almighty even when everything is fine. Have gratitude all the time for His blessings.

Regular prayer and contemplation calm the mind and makes us more confident. One will certainly be able to observe the positive effect.

Follow the Circadian rhythm

The body and mind go through a 24-hour cycle. They are fresh in the early morning hours. For best performance, keep the most important tasks for that time. Long sleep during the daytime and intense work or study late at night is against the normal pattern of our autonomic nervous system and hormones.

Respect the body clock and plan your daily routines accordingly.

Stay connected with old friends

Friends made during childhood and young age are precious. They often know us better than others. The bonds need to be nurtured. Even if they are at a distance, do not forget to speak to old pals from time to time and on special days like their birthday and anniversaries.

The pleasure of meeting up and talking to old friends is unmatched.

Look for an opportunity in the adversity

Some adverse circumstances will come in our life from time to time. We must not get emotionally disturbed or dejected. Never lose confidence and do not curse or blame yourself. Look for a solution and a way to get out of it.

Often hardship brings out the best in us and makes one try things differently and better.

Shun promotional health claims

People are often swayed by advertisements asserting rapid health benefits of commercial food supplements which have no evidence. It could be energy boosters, protein shakes, plant extracts and products that claim to slow ageing.

Stay away from false claims, and avoid indiscriminate use of multivitamins, pain killers and sleep medicines.

Be liberal with appreciation

Everyone likes to be appreciated. Have no inhibition to express admiration when you are impressed by anyone's skill or positive action. It costs nothing but gives happiness to others and encourages them.

Provided it is genuine, it is good to acknowledge and praise even relatively small things like smart appearance, tasty cooking and simple social acts.

Growth is always collective

Unlike the beautiful lotus flower that blooms alone in the mud, progress or growth in life does not occur in isolation. Mutual support and upliftment enable people to prosper collectively.

One cannot climb up by pulling people down. Help others thrive. We will grow when those around us also grow.

Get happiness from simple acts

Just recall how you felt after exercising, eating healthy food, doing yoga, participating in a game, visiting a religious place, watering a plant, feeding a child or helping someone in need. The common factor of such actions is that they are simple but satisfying.

Simple positive activities make us feel good; why not do them more regularly.

Avoid acts that we may regret later

At times we do certain acts carelessly, only to wish later that we had been more cautious. Some examples are overeating, overspending, missing a deadline, back biting and saying something hurtful. They leave a bad feeling and make one regret later.

Being conscious of the potential undesirable consequences of negative actions helps to avoid them.

Nurture all relationships

At times we take our close family members like spouse, parents, children and siblings for granted. All relationships need nurturing. Simple expressions of love and affection will surely give them pleasure. After all, we also feel good when they make such gestures to us.

Do not forget to routinely extend courtesies to near and dear ones, to show them that you care.

Some things are best left unsaid

Generally, it is good to express what is in the mind. However, some issues and matters are obvious and need not be conveyed, especially if they are unpleasant or distressing. Rubbing in someone's failure or shortcomings can only spoil the mood and the relationship.

It is better to remain quiet than to use hurtful and unkind words.

READERS NOTE

Well known facts also need to be reiterated

We are all aware that regular exercise, diet rich in fruits and vegetables, mental relaxation, yoga and meditation are beneficial for health. Similarly, most of the ideas in this book are well known, but have been expressed so that they remain in our consciousness and are translated into action.

Good ideas need to be reminded!

People behave the same in similar circumstances

Someone who is supportive, sincere, honest, committed and loyal will always be the same. Another individual who cheats, deserts in a crisis, tells lies or betrays trust even once will repeat it in similar circumstances.

The basic nature, thoughts and instincts of a person do not change much over time.

Be a good role model for youngsters

Young people subconsciously imbibe the habits and traits of their parents, teachers and elders. Over time, the repeated exposure to the pattern of behavior becomes ingrained in them, even if they dislike or resist some of the aspects.

Being a good role model is the best way to mold youngsters.

A smile is the best greeting

A smile is the most warm and pleasant expression. This nonverbal greeting makes the other person comfortable and feel welcome. It puts them at ease, and further communication is facilitated. The magical effect of a smile is instantly evident.

Develop the lovely habit of smiling and enjoy the rapport and reciprocation.

Being in doubt is the most stressful

Situations in which there is dilemma between two options are disturbing and stressful. Once we decide on one path, the tension disappears as we get occupied in following it with certainty. Even in normal and pleasant circumstances, being in doubt can make us uneasy.

Decisiveness and clarity of thought alleviate stress.

All requests need not be accommodated

Sometimes we get an unreasonable request which is difficult to fulfill. At the same time, we do not want to upset the person by refusing. In such a quandary, it is better to say a polite 'no' than having to do something which is not right.

One should be courteous and helpful to others but must not agree to any action at the cost of ethics and principles.

Positive attitude is the best virtue

Many factors determine the value or success of an individual in an organization. These attributes include education, intelligence, skills, discipline, work ethics, dependability, hard work, creativity, commitment and attitude.

All virtues are important but the most important is a positive attitude that draws the best out of the other attributes.

Let the work speak

We cannot cover faults and errors in our actions with words, howsoever smartly we might think we can. Hollow explanations and justifications will not be able to defend them. Hence, we should pay attention to and focus on what we do. The results will follow.

Let genuine and good work speak for itself.

Adapt to the changing world

The internet, digital space and social media have become an integral part of our life in recent times. Technological advancements and innovations will keep taking place. An open mind and a desire to keep learning help in keeping up to date.

We have to move with the world, otherwise we will be left behind.

Creativity gives happiness

Whenever we create anything, like a piece of art or a technical innovation, it gives satisfaction. It may be as diverse as a physical object, painting, writeup, culinary dish or any form of a new system.

Creativity reflects intelligence and imagination. Besides other dividends, it is a great source of pleasure.

Growth is a pleasure to witness

Watching, supporting and facilitating growth gives a positive feeling. It could be a natural process like a growing child, pet or even a plant. It may also be related to a man-made entity like a physical structure, project or even an organization.

Whether we are participants or just observers, growth elicits fascination, awe and wonder.

Do not be over-inquisitive about others

There are aspects of one's life and issues which one may not like to discuss or reveal at a given time. We should avoid being intrusive in the private matters of other people. By being over-inquisitive we may end up offending or putting off the person.

Unless someone wants to talk about their problem, you should not probe into personal issues of others.

Parents are the best well wishers

Youngsters sometimes feel that they can watch their own interest and that parents are too strict or over-controlling. This is a big misconception which they always repent later.

No one can wish as much good for anyone as the parents do. It is the surest and purest love that exists in the world.

The art of parenting

Parenting is an art and a skill. Unfortunately, it is not formally taught to young couples. Being gentle yet firm is an essential component. Clear messages must be given to children in terms of what is expected of them and what is permitted.

Without being rough or too strict, the boundaries of acceptable behavior and activities of the child must be defined and ensured.

Prioritize

We often have to face multiple problems at a given time. It is not possible to deal with all the issues simultaneously and we need to decide how to tackle them serially for the best possible outcome. Our approach should depend on the relative urgency and importance of the tasks.

Especially when time is a constraint, prioritization is very important.

Invest in systems

It is true that an institution is as good or as bad as the personnel working there. However, people come and go but proper processes, once laid down, sustain and maintain the ethos of the organization.

To make an organization stable and strong we need to create and follow good, transparent, ethical and progressive protocols.

Good ideas must reach the top person

Subordinates hesitate to communicate suggestions to the top person in an organization because they do not want to break the protocol. Many good ideas go waste as they do not reach the decision maker who could appreciate and implement them.

It is the responsibility of the leader to create a friendly and open atmosphere that will facilitate exchange of ideas.

If you want change, do something about it

We keep noting things around us that we feel should change. Unfortunately, most people expect things to happen without any real contribution from their side. A major issue may indeed be beyond one individual.

Setting an example by taking even small steps for bringing out change may influence others to follow suit!

Avoid cribbing and criticizing all the time

Those who grumble over small issues and keep criticizing people or situations actually harm themselves only. It soon becomes a habit, and one keeps finding fault with everything. This catches up on the general mood and reflects in the personality.

People who remain positive are happy and at peace with themselves and the world.

Do not take extreme steps in haste

Quitting a job, breaking a relationship or going to court are extreme decisions which change the course of life. Do not let ego, impulsiveness, lack of communication or external interference lead to such irreversible steps that can cause pain and regret later.

Discuss vexatious matters with someone trustworthy and take action only if convinced that one will be more at peace afterwards.

Change only if it is clearly for the better

At times we do not appreciate what we have and want a change since something else looks more attractive. This could be our job, place of living or routine things like a vehicle, household equipment or club.

Change may make life more interesting. However, consider what added value and comfort it will bring.

Prayer always gives us peace

While praying, submit to God with total humility and faith. Instead of specifying exactly what is personally desired, simply surrender to God's will. In fact, when we pray for the welfare of others, it gives us greater joy and contentment.

Praying with the belief that everything happens for a reason is a source of great tranquility and serenity.

Do not bite the hand that feeds

We should be committed to the place we work in. In fact, the character of a person can be judged from his or her loyalty and sincerity. Anyone with integrity, ethics and conscience will be fully devoted to the system to which one belongs.

People who have a bad mouth, cheat or go against the interest of their own workplace cannot be trusted for anything.

Do not be dogmatic

The more we know, the more we know that we know less. As we keep learning, it is soon realized that we are only scratching the surface of knowledge. Science teaches us that what is true today might be challenged and proved wrong tomorrow.

Avoid being dogmatic and always keep the mind open.

Experts need to commit

Anyone who consults a professional like a doctor, chartered accountant, architect, lawyer or counsellor expects clear advice on the right course to be taken.

As the best-informed person on the subject, the expert should give a definite opinion instead of playing safe and being non-committal.

The best advice comes from the expert

It is strange when someone comes for advice from a professional such as a doctor, and then ignores it in favor of the suggestions of relatives, friends, neighbors or colleagues. Preferring the opinion of a lay person over that of a master of the subject defies logic.

It is wise to follow expert advice.

Common sense is a must for all professions

To be successful in any profession we need to be well informed about our subject, be abreast of the latest developments and have adequate experience. However, knowledge must be combined with common sense. Factors such as local circumstances, laws and obstacles all need to be kept in mind.

As they say, "Think globally but act locally".

Learn to accept

Just because something is unfamiliar or not in line with our thinking, we should not reject it. Anything that is legal, ethical and morally good should be acceptable. We need to be less judgmental or rigid and should have an open mind for this to happen.

An attitude of non-acceptance is a common source of stress.

Beware of staying in the limelight

One may feel nice and important to be in the limelight and soak in the attention being received. However, when someone is in constant focus, the faults and mistakes are also highlighted along with the person's brilliance. The longer it continues, the more uncomfortable it tends to become.

Public scrutiny can be very disconcerting!

Develop oratory skills

For public speaking, prepare well and jot down points but do not read out a written speech. Feel the pulse of the moment, develop rapport with the audience, cater to all its levels, express the message clearly and never overstep the allotted time. Make the beginning and the end impressive.

Oratory skills are an asset and can be developed by practice.

Don't give advice unless it is sought

If you perceive that a friend is facing a problem, make yourself available for any help. However, do not thrust suggestions on how to deal with the issue, as they may not be appropriate. Even though we may mean well, giving unsolicited advice may be taken as unnecessary intrusion into personal matters.

If anyone needs advice let him or her ask for it.

Visualize the long-term effects of decisions

While making decisions in important or complicated matters, think of the possible consequences of each option. Consider the positive as well as the potential negative implications in the short, medium and long term.

Do not fall for merely the immediate gains of your actions, howsoever attractive they may appear to be.

Tackle a problem by talking to yourself

To solve your own problems, step away mentally and try talking to yourself as if to a third person. It then becomes easier to think clearly, analyze the situation in an objective manner and generate rational options without being influenced too much by emotion.

We are generally very good at giving advice to others... why not counsel ourself too!

The 'true self' is revealed in a crisis

One is often not able to judge people in normal circumstances. It is during extraordinary conditions that the level of maturity, stability, rationality and decision-making ability of a person are revealed.

Just as a sailor's abilities are best tested in a storm, crisis situations bring out one's real self.

Do one task at a time

Our brain cannot perform more than one complex cognitive work at a given moment. If we attempt multitasking, we actually toggle between the tasks at fleeting intervals. The result is compromised efficiency and output.

It is better to devote complete attention to one piece of work for a reasonable period before shifting focus to another.

Meditation techniques

There are many forms of meditation with different techniques and procedures. They include Mindfulness, Spiritual, Focused, Movement, Mantra recitation, Transcendental, Progressive, Loving-kindness and Visualization meditation.

One can try out these methods and choose the one, or more, that are suitable and comfortable. They all serve the same purpose.

Consciously feed positivity to the subconscious mind!

The subconscious mind is a faithful follower of the conscious mind. It accepts whatever information and directions are passed on to it without question or doubt and starts working on it.

If one chooses to believe that one is healthy, happy and peaceful, the subconscious mind miraculously ensures that it is brought to reality.

Practice all limbs of yoga!

Yoga does not imply just physical posture. There are 8 limbs or stages. These are Yama (restraints), Niyama (self-discipline), Asana (postures), Pranayama (breathing techniques), Pratyahara (withdrawal of senses), Dharana (concentration), Dhyana (meditation) and Samadhi (absorption).

The more stages we can cover, the closer we come to enlightenment and bliss.

Laughter is definitely the best medicine

A good laugh is the cheapest and most freely available healer. It immediately lightens the mood, relieves stress and promotes a sense of well-being. One does not need to crack a great joke for it. Finding ordinary things funny is enough to brighten the day.

Laughing together is especially effective in striking a pleasant chord between people.

Do what is right without bothering what others say

Sometimes we worry too much about what others will say or think. Of course we should be doing things in a socially acceptable manner, but that should not be the sole aim and purpose of our deeds. No one can please the whole world.

Do what is morally and ethically right, and gives satisfaction, peace and happiness. Do not place excessive value on others' opinions.

Self-pity is disabling, destructive and debilitating

Self-pity, despair, helplessness and resignation are negative feelings. They tend to justify situations and pacify us transiently. However, they are self-propagating and prevent us from conquering pessimism.

Do not wallow in self-pity. Instead of feeling sorry for yourself, get over weak moments with willpower, self-belief and by consciously taking positive steps to emerge stronger.

The middle path

The middle path is the best to take, be it balance between work and enjoyment, family and job, exercise and relaxation, introversion and extroversion, etc. Too much indulgence in something is bad while too much avoidance can make life insipid.

It is wise to set your own limits and avoid extremes in whatever you do.

Avoid the stress factors in daily life

Stress is usually self-created. It occurs when we try to hide something, leave a task incomplete, offend or make someone upset, are unable to make a decision, go against our conscience, or pursue unhealthy activities that make us feel guilty.

The best way to avoid stress is to keep busy and do activities that give satisfaction.

Words may not be consistent with deeds

Words are reflections of a suggestion, assurance, promise, advice or appreciation. These may be genuine or could be hollow. Never judge someone only by words. Watch whether actions match the statements.

With experience and insight one can make the right judgment about the reliability of what someone says.

Revenge and retaliation start a cycle

A desire to take revenge from someone who has wronged us is one of the most long-lasting negative feelings. The injury caused may have been bad, but wanting to get even is worse. It could even start a cycle of hostility and damaging actions.

If one cannot forgive, just forget and move on in life.

Drop negative feelings

Jealousy, anger and hatred are self-damaging. By harboring these we give too much importance to the actions of others and let them influence our psyche. These negative feelings prevent us from fruitfully using our time and energy.

Do not let feelings be unduly dictated by the behavior of others. Learn to 'let go'.

Etiquettes earn respect

Good manners are a reflection of upbringing, education and social sense. A polite person with etiquette will always be liked by everyone. Decent behavior under all circumstances shows inner strength and self-control.

Always remain courteous, even if someone is being rude, brash, assertive or insulting.

Showing 'attitude' does not help the cause

When things are going fine, luck is shining and plans are showing good results, let the smooth run continue and take you to the pinnacle of success. Arrogance can create obstacles in the process.

Realize that if we show haughtiness and start acting pricey when we are doing well, the progress can derail.

Better things may be in store

Things may not go our way at times even when we put in our best effort. Destiny may be taking us on an even better path to our goal! In fact, if one looks back, most good things that happened to us were probably not planned.

We hardly know what is best for us in the long run. Do not prematurely start blaming luck for any setback.

Respect regional practices

Every region in the world has a different lifestyle regarding dressing, eating, and social behavior which are peculiar to that place. Practices vary and have their own charm. When we travel or migrate to somewhere new, we should have regard for the local customs, accept them and try to pick them up.

Always have respect for local traditions of any place.

Do not compare with others

When we compare ourselves to others, we undermine our identity and uniqueness. Every person has a set of factors and circumstances which dictate who one is and what one has become. Respect individuality! Nature intends everyone to be different.

If comparison must be made, it should be with one's own self every day to keep improving and evolving a better version.

Do not be disturbed by minor issues

If we let little things upset us, we spoil our day and are not able to perform to our potential. There will always be minor irritants in life which should not be paid too much attention. Everything will not go our way and we should learn to accept aberrations.

Response to a problem must be proportional. Small problems need a small response only!

Looking 'within' is important

If something is brought closer than the 'near point' of our vision, it becomes blurred. Indeed, if an object is too close to us, we may not be able to even identify it. Perhaps that is why, symbolically, we remain oblivious of what is within us.

Focusing inward is more difficult than looking outwards.

Listen to the elders

As we mature, we start realizing that many things we had considered important were not really so. Those we ignored or took for granted could be the ones of actual value. The earlier this understanding happens, the better.

Talking to senior people allows us to imbibe their wisdom and learn from their experience.

Response to mental stress is physical too

When man lived in jungles, physical threat caused a 'fight or flight' response by sympathetic nervous system activation leading to fast heartbeat, sweating, rise in blood pressure and increased blood flow to muscles. These changes prepared the person to deal with the challenge.

Present day acute mental stress causes the same sympathetic physical response, but it serves no useful purpose.

Regular meditation has long term benefits

Enjoyment through pleasurable activities can provide relief to an agitated mind, but the benefits are short lived. Meditation, on the other hand, when practiced regularly, provides long term benefits.

Pleasure is transient and tends to rebound to an unpleasant distraught state, but the effects of meditation gradually evolve into a state of peace, calmness and bliss.

Express what is in your mind

Do not presume that the other person knows what is in your mind. Sometimes the fear of upsetting the other person makes us hesitate to say the right thing. However, lack of communication is even worse.

The art and skill of polite, clear and honest communication is learnt by paying attention to it and through regular practice.

Use power naps

Most of us work long hours every day. It is important to take short periods of rest in between. Take an afternoon nap of 15-20 minutes. One can individualize it to any time according to the day's schedule. It is refreshing and can-do wonders for the rest of the day.

On a busy day, a brief period of relaxation and a nap are always rejuvenating.

Stay away from health fads

From time-to-time different health fads catch the attention of people, like keto diet consisting of only proteins, very low-calorie diets or high intensity exercise schedules. Such drastic methods are attractive but risky, unscientific and non-sustainable.

The human body cannot become healthy by adopting sudden and extreme changes.

Put in the best in whatever you do

Whenever we undertake any project, examination, job or task, we should put in our best effort with sincerity. The results are likely to be favorable. Even if we are not successful, there will be no regrets. Ultimately, we are answerable only to our own self.

The regret of not having toiled enough bothers more than the failure itself.

Have preventive health checkups

A vehicle, generator and water filter need periodic servicing, an air conditioner needs pre-summer cleaning and so on. The human body is also a machine and needs regular maintenance.

A preventive yearly checkup of any person after the age of 40 will help early detection of health issues and enable timely action.

About the Authors

Dr. Daljit Singh Utaal did MBBS, DCH and MD Paediatrics from CMC, Ludhiana. Had a brilliant academic record with top positions, many awards, distinction and University scholarship.

Did FAIMER, Fellowship at Philadelphia, USA, and visited UK for Fellowship from the Royal College of Physicians - Child Health (RCPCH). For academic, scientific, research, editorial and administrative contributions, has been honoured with Fellowship of Indian Academy of Paediatrics (FIAP), National Neonatal Forum (FNNF), National Academy of Medical Sciences (FAMS), and International Academy of Medical Sciences (FIMSA). As a Clinical Professor, was adjudged 'Best Teacher' by MBBS students.

Authored 5 books on Paediatrics and Medical Education. Gave more than 150 scientific talks, guest lectures, and conducted dozens of workshops and training programs. Was National faculty member of PALS and NALS programs of IAP and NNF.

Held several administrative positions at university level, including Dean of Faculty of Medical Sciences and Member of Senate. Actively contributed to promotion of medical education through many innovative programs at University and National level.

Dr. Gurpreet Singh Wander passed MBBS from Govt. Medical College, Patiala with Honor's. During graduation was awarded Merit Scholarship and 3 Silver Medals. Did MD in Medicine and DM in Cardiology from PGIMER, Chandigarh. Joined DMC&H in 1988 and started the cardiology unit.

Has published 279 research papers, 133 of them in foreign Journals of repute like: The Lancet, Nature Genetics and Journal of American College of Cardiology. Has contributed 84 chapters in books. Chief Editor of 7 textbooks in medicine including The Yearbook of Medicine, Progress in Medicine, Medicine Update, Postgraduate medicine textbook and four books of cardiology. Has been co-supervisor of 52 MD, 18 DM and 4 PhD theses.

Awarded K. Sharan Cardiology Excellence award by IMA India. Dr. B C Roy National Award for the year 2006. Name figured in Guinness Book of World Records for creating the largest vegetable heart mosaic.

President of the Hypertension Society of India for 2012-13. President of the Association of Physicians of India (API) for 2016-17. Director of Physicians Research Foundation (PRF) of API for the year 2022-25.